The Exit of a Titan

Ambassador Ositadinma Anaedu

The Diplomats' Diplomat!

Compiled and Edited by
Fada Onyii Anaedu and Fada Martin Añụsị

© 2021 Paulinus Onyekwelu Anaedu
Pfarrgasse 1
A-4081 Hartkirchen
E-Mail: franaeduop@yahoo.com

Cover design © Sabine Würmer, Hartkirchen, Austria
Cover photo: © Foto Walter, Grieskirchen, Austria

ISBN: 9-783-750-406-698
Production and publishing: BoD - Books on Demand, Norderstedt

Dedicated to
Amaka, Kamtoo and Kosi

Prologue

Osy, A Tribute to Character
Rev. Fr. Ben Ejeh, Venice-Italy

A rare breed you were
In a murky landscape
Dotted with fellows without character.

Tall you strode like a Colossus
Navigating a sea of soulless sharks
With integrity for watchword
And faith as compass
Compromise, to you, a taboo.

Our paths crossed happily
At God's behest in Providence
And ever bound in fraternal love
Til God's love's eternal embrace.

You live on dear Osy
For love and life in God're eternal.

Ambassador Ositadinma Bartholomew Anaedu
A Short Biographical Ode
by
Fada Onyii

Born in Onitsha on December 30, 1955, our parents gave him the name *O si taa dị nma, ọ dịrịzie gaba* meaning: *since it started today to be good, it will continue to be good.* And because the Igbo folk of our parents' time and generation did not give names arbitrarily, the context of this name was that our father, having retired from the Nigeria Police Force, ventured into business, which then started to show signs of growth and promise. Hence, his name was a prayer both for intercessions already answered and for the future of the still young family to which seven younger siblings will be added in addition to his elder sister, Uchem, named after our paternal grandmother. However, everyone knew him as Ositadinma and Osita or Osy for short. His baptismal name, Bartholomew, was rarely used and found only in some official documents like certificates.

When Osy reached school age, our father wanted the best of foundation-education and upbringing for him. Hence, he decided that he be raised by a cousin, who was a teacher, Mr Marcel Obianọ, who lived and taught at Agụleri. It was during his primary school days that the Nigeria-Biafra civil war broke out. Osy was on a visit to the family house in Onitsha when the war reached the threshold of the commercial city. Consequently, he had to evacuate with the rest of the family to seek refuge in our village in Agụlụzigbo.

After the war in 1970, Osy began his secondary school education at Bubendorff Secondary School, Adazi, finishing in 1975. As was customary then, he did his Higher School at the prestigious Dennis Memorial Grammar School (DMGS), Onitsha. It must be noted that his time at DMGS was as remarkable as it was historic because he became the first Higher School student, who did not do all of his secondary school education and the school certificate in DMGS, to be elected as the Students' Union President, a position that was more prestigious than the senior prefect of the school because the senior prefect was usually an appointee of the school authorities, while the president was an elective office. Again for the fact that Osy, a Catholic, was elected as the Students' Union President in a school that represented and still represent the height of academic excellence in Igbo Anglicanism (same was Christ the King College, Onitsha, and still for the Igbo Catholicism), was really epochal and spoke volumes.

Having finished his Higher School, he gained admission into the prestigious University of Nigeria, Nsukka, UNN, where he studied political science, actively engaging in the University Students' Union politics as a member of the Students' Union Council, and graduating in 1982.

After his Youth Service at the National Assembly, Lagos, during the 1982/83 session, he got a job as a reporter and columnist for the Democrat Newspapers, based in Kaduna, in the Northern part of Nigeria. He was at this job for just a few months before he realised his dream of working in the Nigerian Ministry of Foreign Affairs, Lagos, in December 1983. Rising through the ranks, he got his first international posting in 1990 to Hong Kong. In 1993, he returned to Nigeria and was posted to the Protocol of the Presidential Lounge at the Murtala Mohammed International Airport, Lagos, where he worked till his second international posting to the Permanent Mission of Nigeria to the United Nations Headquarters in New York in 1998.

It is pertinent to note here that, after his first marriage collapsed shortly after he came back from Hong Kong, he literally got 'married' to his job for nearly fifteen years. Consequently, all our official and tricky efforts to hook him up with one of our numerous girlfriends (mine and those of my 7 other siblings) proved abortive until we succeeded with Amaka, his present widow and the mother of his two beautiful and highly gifted children, whom he married sacramentally in 2005, having received the canonical annulment of his first marriage more than ten years earlier.

Osy so dedicated himself to his job at the Presidential Lounge that his name became synonymous with the Presidential Lounge of the MMIA such that when postings were being considered again in the ministry, the then Nigerian dictator, General Sani Abacha, personally directed the then Minister of Foreign Affairs, Chief Tom Ikimi, to post him to the United Nations in New York. That was how his carrier at the UN took off and it was at the UN in New

4

York that he honed his negotiating skills as an international diplomat and erudite negotiator.

After this stint at the UN in New York, he returned to Nigeria in 2002 and resumed at the Ministry of External Affairs Headquarters in Abuja. Not quite long afterwards, he received a call from the Office of the then National Security Adviser, Gen. Aliyu Mohammed Gusau to resume at his office. He stayed at the Office of the National Security Adviser to the then President Olusegun Obasanjo until his second stint with the Permanent Mission of Nigeria to the UN in Geneva, Switzerland in 2007, where he worked until his official retirement from the Nigerian Civil Service, having put in the mandatory 35 years of service. However, because of his invaluable experience and expertise, the then Director General of the World Intellectual Property Organisation (WIPO) decided to retain his services at WIPO as his Strategic Adviser, where he finally retired in 2018.

After Osy's retirement from the UN, he devoted his energy and time to something he considered very important to humanity, namely human health. Without being a medical practitioner or having had any formal training in orthodox medicine, Osy used his life health challenges to develop and devote himself to healthy eating practices and techniques.

Because various sicknesses like high blood pressure and diabetes are in our family history, Osy inherited these sicknesses at an early age. I can still remember vividly that, whenever he travelled, his medications always had a separate travelling bag. However, in order to rid himself of so much medication, he had to resort to alternative medicine by changing his eating habit. Although he was never into alcohol, smoking and junk foods, he went an extra mile to start eating organic and mostly vegetables and herbs, with the result that he lost much weight. However, without taking any drugs again, his health so improved that his work rate actually doubled and he rarely fell sick apart from the occasional seasonal flu. From this personal experience, he became so convinced of the efficacy of alternative medicine, that he embarked on a mission to educate anyone he came in contact with on his experienced and researched findings, which he articulated in his opus magnum, a 684-page book on healthy living: *Your Microbiome (Bacteria) is a Wonder of Nature: Activate and Optimize – Eating for Healthy Longevity*, published in 2020. However, I must confess that this obsession with alternative medicine made him lose sight of the need for regular orthodox medical check-ups, because he was rarely sick and always in terrific state of health. He felt absolutely in control of his health. And that was the negative aspect of it. That was why his malignant prostate cancer was not discovered on time until it became too late. This experience can be likened to what Steve Jobs, the founder of Apple, experienced with his pancreatic cancer.

A little digression may be pertinent here because, just like in our family, certain illnesses, like pancreatic cancer, ran in Steve Jobs' family too. When I stumbled on an answer by Leo Chelliah, CEO at Dreamguys Technologies to a question on Steve Jobs' cancer, I found it *ad rem* to how Osy handled his sickness too. Leo Chelliah writes:

From his early life onwards, Steve Jobs was very obsessive about the way he lived, he would do quite a lot of intermittent fasting, juice fasting, prolonged fasting etc., which are actually good ways to improve your body. Based on his official BIO, he actually switched from drinking tea to just drinking really hot water, because it's mostly the same satisfaction you get. If you really try for a couple of days you would know it's actually true. So his obsession with how to live was actually a really good way of living life. However, what went wrong is, when he found out that he had pancreatic cancer, he went deep in thinking of the actual disease and did searches/research as much as possible, and he concluded, that eradicating a disease like cancer would be done right through not cutting yourself, rather doing cleansing and natural remedy to reverse the condition, which actually would have to be the right way of fixing this disease. But our humanity is not yet advanced enough in natural remedies and reversing the condition, and as a whole society, we are obsessed with fixing the disease rather than reversing a disease. Thus rather than accepting the reality that he had to open up his body and fix the disease, he obsessed with reversing the condition. Again there is not enough proof we could reverse cancer right now, but that's what he thought was the right way and obsessed about it.

Actually, Steve Jobs created really good products because of his obsession with how a product should be used, true to its nature, eradicating the unnecessary and making the product true to its use. His obsession with products got us really good products. But his obsession over how a disease could/should be cured, even though it was right in what he was doing, time was not in his favour. Within 9 months of identification, further scans showed the cancer had progressed and it was aggressive. Still, that was for that moment, and due to his obsession, he had struggles accepting the medical ways and kept opposing things which he didn't accept were right, causing his disease to overtake him sooner. That was a man obsessed with doing things right!!!

(cf. https://www.quora.com/If-Steve-Jobs-knew-his-genetics-were-high-for-pancreatic-cancer-why-didn-t-he-search-help-in-the-early-stages?q=steve%20jobs%20pancreat, culled on 20.02.2023)

Unfortunately, this is similar to what happened to Ambassador Ositadinma too. He was absolutely convinced that his methods were working. And, from all indications, which he shared with us in the family, his methods were working; a method that brought down his prostate count from more than 2,000 PSA, when it was first diagnosed in May 2022, to less than 30 PSA count in the first week of December, 2022. However, his condition so dramatically changed in that first week of December that he had to be admitted in the hospital. And on the 11th day of December, on the *Gaudete* Sunday – the Sunday of Joy, it pleased the Lord to call him home and relieve him of the pains and sufferings he was going through. However, that was not before Ujunwa, the baby of the house, was able to organise a priest, Father Conrad Ukozor, who went and administered the last sacraments to him, though at the time of administration, we all had in mind that it was the *Sacrament of the Sick*, because none of us believed at the time that the end had come for him.

I would like to mention here and thank some friends, who cared for him and visited him till the very end: his bosom friend and brother from another womb, Amb. John Chika Ejinaka; Dr Shafiu Adamu Yauri, a very close friend, who was actually the only person allowed to have uninterrupted access to him while in the hospital; a business associate, Uche Obiozor – the owner of the Diplomatic Village, Abuja; my 'son' and bosom friend, Barr. Emeka Orji; his mechanic and driver, David Maiyaki, whom he took as a brother; his two carers Henry Solomon and David Sabo, who cared for him like their own blood. The testimonies of these people, who were with him to the end, testify to how much he wanted to be there for his young family and the equanimity with which he endured his pains. Even the Doctor, who cared for him, Dr. Tina Anya, had this to say in a WhatsApp text to his bereaved wife, Amaka: *Good morning Ma. I have been meaning to call you and offer you my deepest condolences over the passing of your husband, but decided to leave you to be with your family and loved ones.*

*I knew your husband only for a brief period, but he made a huge impression on me, and I won't forget him. I am grateful to God for the opportunity He gave me to help care for **His son** in the last few months of his life. He fought the cancer gallantly, but eventually I guess it was his time to go. He* *wanted to shield you and the children from the pain of watching him deteriorate, but in the process he denied you and himself the opportunity to spend time together before he passed. So sorry for your loss, Ma!*

My prayer is that the Lord continue to comfort you and your family, and grant you every grace and strength you need to be able to move on!

May Ambassador Ositadinma Anaedu rest in perfect peace with the Most High!

God bless you richly Ma!

That Osy lived peacefully and died even more peacefully is not in doubt. The photo of him taken by my sister, Chidinma, who just arrived Abuja from Lagos unannounced on that fateful Sunday morning of December 11, 2022, only to meet his still warm but dead body, is clear testimony to this. A testimony confirmed by Mrs. Nnenna Ottu, our spiritually gifted family-friend and prayer partner, who dreamt of Osy on the 16th of December, 2022. Nnenna was able to put her dream experience into writing: *"Brother Osy appeared to me. I was actually scared but he said I should not be, that he was the one. Though I had seen him only once before, during Chidinma's wedding, I recognized him immediately and I told him that I knew him. The first thing he told me was that he missed knowing me when he was alive but that he was still happy to know me even now that he had gone. He acknowledged the fact that he found out late how much his siblings cared about and loved him, that he didn't know that much when he was alive. He said I should thank them for supporting him with everything especially with their prayers that got him to the good place where he was. He told me that his spirit had left the mortuary and that he was trying to do some things and anything he could do to help his siblings. Even in spirit, he would definitely do that. However, he added that there was a limit to what a spirit could do and urged his siblings to keep praying. He then gave some instructions as to how he would be buried."*

It will be difficult to count the various groups of people, who will definitely miss Ambassador Osita. First is his still very young family: Amaka, Kamtoo and Kosi. Though still very young, the children are maturing both physically and mentally faster than their age. It was Kamtoo, who reminded his mum that she should take consolation from the fact that his dad died on *Gaudete* Sunday – Sunday of Joy because God did not want him to continue suffering. We, his siblings will definitely miss him for the unity and stability he helped establish and nurture in the family because he was a rallying point and the leader in the family. The numerous students Osy helped, in one way or the other, to pay parts of their school fees in the universities through the scholarship scheme he established in the name of our late father, *Onuwuzuligbo* Anaedu, will definitely miss him. The *Uzuamumu* clan will definitely miss him for the yearly cow-protein feast he provided for them. St. Patrick's Catholic Church, Aguluzigbo, will definitely miss him for his financial contributions and otherwise especially during the annual parish harvest and bazaar celebrations.

There is no doubt that Osy is in peace and in heaven. Testimonies abound. And that is our consolation. We can only thank God for the gift of him and the time we had with him.

Ambassador Ositadinma Anaedu at the United Nations

Positions held by Ambassador Ositadinma Anaedu at the UN

- ➢ Chairman Committee
  EXPERT OFFICIALS MEETINGS OF THE G-77, GREATER NEW YORK AREA, Feb 2000 - Nov 2000

- ➢ Vice Chairman Of The Board
  BUREAU OF THE WORLD SUMMIT ON SUSTAINABLE DEVELOPMENT (WSSD), 2000-2002

- ➢ Chairman
  COMMITTEE OF THE WHOLE (COW) COMMITTEE SIXTH SESSION OF THE COP OF THE UNITED NATIONS CONVENTION TO COMBAT DESERTIFICATION, CUBA, 2002 - Sep 2003

- ➢ Chairman
  COMMITTEE OF THE WHOLE (COW) OF THE CONFERENCE OF THE PARTIES TO UN CONVENTION ON DESERTIFICATION, Aug 2003 - Sep 2003

- ➢ Head of International Affairs
  OFFICE OF THE NATIONAL SECURITY ADVISER TO THE PRESIDENT, ABUJA, NIGERIA, Jan 2003

- ➤ Executive Chairman
  WORKING GROUP 1 ON SOUTH-SOUTH COOPERATION OF THE 11th MEETING OF THE INTERGOVERN-MENTAL FOLLOW-UP AN, 2005

- ➤ Committee Chair
  UNITED NATIONS FRAMEWORK CONVENTION ON CLIMATE CHANGE (UNFCCC), 2006 – 2007

- ➤ Senior Negotiator
  THE NIGERIAN DELEGATION IN THE SECOND COMMITTEE OF THE 61st UNGA, 2006 – 2007

- ➤ Executive Vice President
  THE BUREAU OF THE CONFERENCE OF THE PARTIES TO THE UN CON-VENTION ON BIOLOGICAL DIVER-SITY, 2006 – 2008

- ➤ Chairman
  COMMITTEE UNITED NATIONS CON-VENTION ON CLIMATE CHANGE, 2006 – 2016

- ➢ Executive Chairman
  COMMITTEE OF THE WHOLE OF THE 8TH CONFERENCE OF THE PARTIES TO THE UNCCD, 2007 - 2008

- ➢ Senior Project Coordinator
  NIGERIA'S PRESIDENCY OF THE GENERAL ASSEMBLY OF THE WORLD INTELLECTUAL PROPERTY ORGANIZATION (WIPO), 2007 - 2009

- ➢ Chairman Committee
  BUDGET CONTACT GROUP OF THE NINTH SESSION CONFERENCE OF THE PARTIES TO THE CONVENTION ON BIOLOGICAL, May 2008 – Jun 2008

- ➢ Coordinator
  NIGERIA'S PRESIDENCY OF THE HUMAN RIGHT COUNCIL, Jan 2008 – Oct 2009

- ➢ Coordinator
  AFRICAN GROUP ON HUMAN RIGHT COUNCIL, 2008 – 2011

- ➢ Alternated Representative and Coordination
  THE NIGERIA'S PRESIDENCY OF THE UN COUNCIL; Sept 2011 – Sept 2012

- ➢ Strategic Advisor (Office of the Director-General) WORLD INTELLECTUAL PROPERTY ORGANISATION (WIPO), Sept 2012 – Dec 2017

- ➢ Chairman
  BUDGET COMMITTEE OF THE THIRD MEETING OF THE CARTHEGENA PROTOCOL ON BIOSAFETY, 20th July, 2017

Testimonies of Colleagues from the
Nigerian Diplomatic Community

My Eulogy
Ambassador John Chika Ejinaka.

It is with pain that I write this eulogy for my brother, Ositadinma Anaedu. I can see your face; I still recollect the agony in all our faces. Those last three days before the bell tolled that late Sunday morning. It was painful to all of us, David, Henry, Ngoo and your good friend Uche, owner of the Abuja Diplomatic Village. We watched you writhing in pain. We saw the courage. Yes, I know you wanted to say something. You wanted to talk to me. Yes, each time I called you in my usual way, you tried to respond, but after some efforts, I noticed a feeling of resignation.

We had exchanged greetings the week before while I was in the village for the funeral of my father. You had called to find out about my trip and the state of my arrangements. And when I enquired about your health, in your usual manner you assured me that you were getting better and that the pains on your leg had stopped. But underneath, your voice betrayed those pretenses. You never wanted anybody to share in your pains. You could then imagine how I panicked when the following week, David called to inform me that your health got worse and Ngoo came with an ambulance and you were on admission in the hospital.

Osy Anaedu had been my friend and brother for over 42years. Right from the first time we drew closer as students at the University of Nigeria, Nsukka, to our orientation camp at the University of Ibadan for the National Youths Service. You later got cross-posted to Lagos, where you were deployed to the National Assembly for the service year while I remained at the University of Ibadan, having been deployed to the Department of Modern Languages for my primary assignment. It was not surprising when at the conclusion of our youths' service, destiny brought us together once again in the then Ministry of External Affairs. I recall our reaction and the warm embrace with which we welcomed ourselves to the Foreign Ministry. Since then, everybody knew us as brothers, only separated by our different surnames.

But Osy, you were a very nice person, very humble, compassionate and very caring, always ready to help and the first to avoid anything that could result in conflict. Your commitment to work was very legendary. Your passion for excellence became noticed at those early stages by no other than the erudite Ambassador Ejor Abuah. Though a very senior Ambassador at the time, he was known for his strict commitment to excellence. He saw you as a perfect match, little wonder that he requested for your deployment to his office and took you as a personal assistant in the Inter-African Affairs department.

Your interaction with Ambassador Abuah opened the floodgate towards your future engagement in multilateral diplomacy where you excelled to become a major expert and forming part of the Nigerian delegation to major conferences where your expertise was in high demand. I recall your avid contribution to the Nigerian delegation during preparations for the World Summit on Sustainable Development held in Durban South Africa in 2002 and some years later in Rio de Janeiro Brazil. Your participation in the preparatory processes of the United Nations Forum on Forest. You were Nigeria Expert on G77 and China, where you also directed expert discussions as the chair of the expert group, in particular formulating the group's position on the United Nations Framework Convention on Climate Change. At the Human Rights Council in Geneva, you remained a major expert while defending the interest of developing countries. It was therefore not surprising that with your multilateral knowledge, most of your postings in the Ministry revolved between the Permanent Mission of Nigeria New York and Geneva respectively.

I recall that after you finished your tour in Geneva and getting ready to return home to Nigeria, it happened to be the time that Nigeria was elected to the United Nations Security Council. The Nigerian Permanent Representative at the time made a passionate representation to the leadership of the Ministry that you be cross posted to New York to assist with the work of the Security Council. There you remained an active member of the Nigerian team working directly with the Permanent Representative. It was from New

York that you retired from service after your assignment and having completed 35years of service.

It was 35years of meritorious service to father
land, one that was cherished by all that came across
you. But you were not done yet; your good work followed you when, on retirement in 2015, the then Director General World International Properties Organization reached out to you and appointed you as
a Senior Special Assistant in the organization. You
had, while covering WIPO as one of your schedules
in the Nigerian Permanent Mission in Geneva, made
lasting impression on the WIPO Director General,
which compelled him to strive to bring you into the
organization. You remained in that position as a staff
of the organization until you finally retired from active service.

Mr. FRESH, that was what my wife and children
used to call you, I recall those days when you used to
be our guest in Geneva. You preferred fresh fruit
juice, instead of the already canned or bottled juice
that remain common features in most supermarkets
then in Geneva, then preference for steamed vegeta-
ble and half-done Okra soup. Each time you visited
for one conference or the other from Nigeria, my
wife was very disposed to giving you those special
treatment that before long we started sharing in
those preferences. You could then imagine what the
reaction of my children was, though now grown,
when the news of your sudden departure reached
them in their present abode in Maryland. Even my

wife whom I had often updated about your health situation, shared in their expression of shock and disbelieve. You, in fact, left a lasting legacy as you just published a well-researched book on eating healthy, which, to many, was a total digression from your multilateral habit.

When I reflect over your life, the much I knew about you, those many sleepless nights working to come up with quality paper for the next UN meeting, those sleepless nights negotiating the African position, speaking on behalf of Nigeria, sitting and talking some till early morning the following day, looking at your lifeless body, the question that came to my mind was why all these struggles. Yes Osy, when you were wheeled out from the theatre where you were taken for x-ray and other procedures, back to the emergency ward in that Garki Hospital, when your friend Uche drew my attention to your lifeless body. Yes, David and Henry shedding tears, as I touched your body which was still warm, your face this time was glowing, I noticed a kind of peace in you. Yes, the suffering of those last days was over. Although I still thought you would soon wake up fully healed and strong, as I continued holding you with supplication in my heart, but then I felt that your body was gradually getting cold. It then dawned on me that you have returned home to your maker. He alone knows when it is time for the bell to toll.

Adieu my dear brother, Osy. I know you are now in heaven. Left for you, you would have remained for those your lovely children, for your wife, Amaka, and for all of us. Surely, you fought, you prayed; many times we prayed together, you did all that was humanly possible, but to God you belong and to Him you have returned.

May your soul rest in peace. Amen!

Osita, How I wished I had Supernatural Powers!
Dr. Shafiu Adamu Yauri

We have always been together, in good times and in challenging times. The loss of a friend like you is something that I can never recover from. You have accomplished many good things in life. Your passing away is not something easy to get over. It is a shock that's difficult to come to terms with. It's sad to realize that my good friend, His Excellency Ambassador Ositadinma Anaedu, is gone; that we shall see no more. However, I am consoled by the saying that true friendship doesn't die but lives on in the hearts. Hence, my pen has given me the opportunity through this tribute to express my true feelings in words, in the fond memories of what we went through in life.

We are consoled that you fought a brave and strong battle, but the sickness would not allow you to get better. You took each day in your stride, never really complaining, always feeling tired but always hoping that the treatments would finally work so you could get on with life. This was my hope too.

Osita, you are a good man inside and out, a wonderful friend to me, supporting me for over 20 years with good pieces of advice and exhortations, kind words and encouragements. One of your beliefs in life was the importance of being authentic with people, saying what needs to be said because it's good for people to be real (I know you were greatly misunderstood on account of this even by colleagues, bosses and peers). Unfinished businesses caused you pain and being misunderstood even greater pain, yet you trudged on. Also I always admired how you never judged or forced your opinions on anyone, but offered valuable and truthful advice that I will surely miss. I hope you forgive me for the times I brushed you off when you talked about the possibility of dying. I just wanted to keep your spirit up so I always told you that you would be okay and not to worry.

Osita, you served as a bridge builder for the Nigerian Delegation to the United Nations Office in New York and to the United Nations Office in Geneva when you served as an Official of the Permanent Mission of Nigeria to the United Nations. In addition to these "official" roles, you were also the Chief Host and Overseer of the Nigerian Delegation to all WIPO, Human Rights, Migration and Health matters meetings and engagements of Nigeria at the UN in Geneva. It is to your credit that Nigeria scored all the golden goals and diplomatic triumphs in IGC (*Inter-Governmental Consultations* on Migration, Asylum and

Refugees), Develop new Agenda and Technical Assistance and Capacity Building programs that Nigeria attracted from several UN Agencies in Geneva. This culminated to your appointment as Technical Assistant to the Director General WIPO in Geneva.

Do you know what? Sometimes I wish I had supernatural powers to bring you back so we could talk again and share moments as we've always done. But alas, I know this will never be. You are gone. But your memory will always remain fresh in my life. Now you are gone. I pray for your departed soul! And with deep sorrow in my heart, I bid you farewell.

Goodbye to a Titan
Ambassador Lilian Onoh.

Sometimes in life, God brings unique people across your path that makes you pause in wonder at his creation. Osita Anaedu was one such people.

I met him during my first posting to the United Nations in New York and unlike others who offered no help, he took me by the hand to the UN, showed me the bewildering maze that I would have to work in and how to operate in it. I followed him to my first negotiation session. He was the person who taught me a simple maxim – *"You will never get everything you want, so try to ensure you and others get what you can live with."* With this maxim, I was able to succeed for all future negotiations I had to do and I never forget to say a quiet *"Thank you"* to him for that life lesson.

At the UN, I discovered that he was unbeatable. He was beloved by the delegates from different parts of the world because of his authenticity. He was totally politically incorrect. But he always delivered his politically incorrect points by attributing it to his "*village upbringing*". And with that, he made everybody laugh when others would make the same points and elicit rancour.

He trained all the junior staff that came across his path without holding back the immense knowledge and skills in his arsenal. He was generous with dispersing knowledge – the most precious gift to give another human being.

Nigeria and every developing country owe this man an incalculable debt. Without any direction from anybody, Ositadinma Anaedu looked at the sorry state of developing countries and the stupidity of corrupt individuals stashing their money in developed countries instead of using the funds to develop their countries and decided to do what nobody else had dared before namely: *He decided to demand the return of stolen funds back to countries of origin!*

It was audacious and almost like a pipe dream. And until he decided to do so, it seemed totally impossible that Western Countries – the choice destination for Nigeria's looted funds – would ever return the funds. But try Osy did. And succeed he did. Beyond even the wildest expectations, he drafted a resolution and gave me the privilege of a minor contribution and then proceeded to pull off the impossible

– the adoption of a resolution at *First Presentation*. And the rest is now history. Without that foundational document, no developing country would have been able to demand the return of funds stolen by corrupt officials which are stashed away overseas.

Osy's achievement is monumental and a historical landmark. In any other country, he would be the recipient of National Honours and multiple awards. He would be an icon. But in our own country, those benefitting from his work would rather not remember that someone did the work that enables them to get billions of Dollars returned to Nigeria.

But God, who created him for a specific purpose has not forgotten him. He did the work he was created to do for the betterment of humanity. He finished the work God gave him to do on earth. His family has lost a beloved brother, husband and father. We, his colleagues have lost a steadfast colleague and friend. Nigeria has lost an unsung hero. But Heaven has gained a most beloved son, to whom God will surely say: *"Well Done, Good and Faithful Servant. Enter Into Your Rest."*

And I say, enjoy your well-deserved rest, my friend and brother. You did well!

Ambassador Lillian Onoh on Ambassador Ositadinma Anaedu in an interview by Christian Ogadibe in *The Sun Newspapers* of March 29, 2020

Christian: How long have you worked in the foreign ministry and what indelible footprints have you left in the sands of time during these years in the service?

Ambassador Lillian: I've been with the Ministry for over 27 years now, to the glory of God because without Him, I do not believe that I could have stayed so long with the service. In terms of achievements, I have to mention three particular things that I will look back upon with great pride: one is when I was a third secretary in New York, my senior colleague in the 2nd Committee, Osita Anaedu, came up with a draft for the return of illegally stolen loot to countries of origin. When he showed it to me, I made some contributions to the draft and without informing HQ or the Head of Mission, we proceeded with the draft to the UN – first to the African Group before then taking it to the G77. Finally we took it to WEOG – Western European and Other Groups – the countries where most of the money was stashed. With all their opposition to the draft, mainly concerning corrupt diversion of returned funds and, of course, a natural reluctance to lose such a lucrative source of funds in their banking system, we were able to have that draft resolution passed in one session – a feat that Nigeria had never before achieved. That Resolution – UN Resolution 55/188 – is the foundational document which enables Nigeria to request the return of illegally stashed loot and has led to the return of billions of dollars to Nigeria from multiple countries.

My second pride (and most probably my best achievement, if you ask me) was my consular work in Togo. When I first got to Togo, the Mission didn't do any consular work and I then took it upon myself to start going to the Prison to find out about the Nigerians being held there. At that time, there were about 180 of them. Through persistence, I was able to get their names and the crimes they had committed only to discover that many were being held for no reason at all. I remember one unfortunate man who had been locked up for over three years because he had recommended a driver who later had an accident with his employer's car and ran away. The employer, in frustration, locked up this poor man and that was how a hardworking man spent three years in jail without charge or trial for nothing! To cut a long story short, with God's incredible grace, I was able to have the man and over 50 prisoners freed within a period of three months. Over the course of the remainder of my stay, I was able to have an additional 50 or more freed – some after trial that sentenced them to fewer years than they had already served in jail. There was a day that a particular Nigerian prisoner – Sani – was freed after five and a half years in jail. We had just left the court where his sentence of three years for stealing a car side-mirror was given and I found myself being cheered by a whole group of Togolese prisoners. Not understanding their joy, I asked the driver what was happening and he told me that since I had Sani tried and freed, the other seven Togolese men who had been arrested with Sani for the side-mirror theft were also free at last. I almost cried for joy that day. Truly, to see each prisoner walk free was always an emotional experience for me. I convinced the Charge d'Affaires that the Mission had to pay their transportation all the way to their home state and give them something to go home with. I know that truly, God was in charge because without prayer, I do not believe I would have been able to go through the gruelling processes required to free each prisoner. In this, as in everything else, I bow to my Lord and Saviour, Jesus Christ.

The third thing that I feel proud of was being Nigeria's chief negotiator for the South Summit Declaration during the Havana Summit of 2000. I was a mere Third Secretary and it was an enormous responsibility to have been given. I must have done it well because before the end of the Summit, I had a job offer from the UN in Geneva, but I didn't want to move – either to the UN or to Geneva.

During the Summit, which was attended by so many Heads of State and Presidents, it was dizzying just watching them pass and identify who was who, I had the incredible privilege of meeting President Fidel Castro and even took a picture with him! Till tomorrow, that remains an indelible experience and if you've never watched President Castro speak, you should find any of his speeches on YouTube and see a true-born orator at work. There have been many other achievements over the years, but these three make me very happy to remember. Even now, each time that Nigeria recovers stolen money from any country, I feel a great sense of pride, knowing that I had a great deal to do with it being possible.

Goodness is Good
Ambassador Abdulwahab, MNI

The transition of our beloved Ambassador Ositadinma Anaedu was painful and heart-breaking. It was a great loss to the nation, to his family and to me personally.

Ositadinma, as I used to call him, worked with me when I was Chief of Protocol at the Presidential Lounge, Lagos. He was one of the six distinguished gallant Protocol Officers, who supported and assisted me to sanitize the protocol services at Murtala Mohammed International Airport, Lagos. He stood by me until we succeeded in defeating the gang of corrupt officers from the Customs, Immigration, FAAN and their Protocol collaborators who were finally removed from the airport. He was not only an illustrious citizen of Nigeria, he was a patriotic and detribalized Nigerian. He was a strong personality with a great spirit to confront challenges and overcome them. He was an achiever with great determination to succeed always. He was responsible, reliable and dependable, a dynamic, seasoned career diplomat full of initiatives, energy and versatility. He was good, the man was really good.

When my daughter got married in New York in 2004, he was in charge of the protocol arrangements and logistics. He also doubled up as the MC. Watching that video again reminds me of his charismatic personality and impeccable King's English. He was a great asset to the Nigerian Foreign Service and also to his community. Our prayers and thoughts are with his loved ones.

My Beloved Ositadinma, you will always have a place in my heart. May the Most Compassionate God rest your soul in everlasting peace and comfort! Amen!

Nigerian Foreign Service Hall of 'Fame
Ambassador Ayo Olukanni

It's indeed heart rending, sad and shocking to hear of the sudden passing away of Ambassador Osita Anaedu. We have known ourselves in the Ministry from when he joined the Foreign Service, but got closer when I joined the team at the Permanent Mission to New York to strengthen the Mission in 2000. This was when, on return to Civil Rule in 1999, Nigeria was literally dragged to become the Chair of the New York Chapter of the G77 & China in 2000. The UN was preparing for the Millennium Summit and the MDGs (Millennium Development Goals). At the same time, G77 & China was preparing for the first ever South Summit held in Havana that year from 10th - 14th April 2000. Osita (or just 'Sita' as he was fondly referred to in New York) was literally at the Centre of the preparatory activities of the G77 for the major meetings of the MILLENNIUM SUMMIT. So much devolved on him as the officer on the Second Committee from the Nigerian Mission to Chair the various Groups of the G77 in preparation for negotiations with other Groups EU, JUCANZ etc. within the UN on the MDGs. He showed himself as a brilliant Diplomat and Multilateralist. And the entire members of delegation from Member States on the 2nd Committee had tremendous respect for him. He covered environmental issues including the UN Forum on Forest and was indeed a force to be reckoned with on discussions in the field of Environment and Sustainable Development generally including thematic areas such as Climate Change, Land Degradation, Air Pollution, Biodiversity, Chemicals etc. It is also on record that on behalf of the G77, he played a significant role in the successful negotiations of the UN Millennium Declaration and Millennium Development Goals. Equally significant was his role in the preparation and adoption of the Havana Declaration and Havana Programme of Action adopted in Havana in April 2000 at the First Ever South Summit.

At the level of Experts, He chaired the negotiations when preparations started in New York and when it continued in Havana. He was there to serve as a guide to the Ministerial segment as well. All of these he did in preparation for the Summit Segment. When the documents were presented to the G77

Heads of State, there was very little to add. G77 members in New York and other Chapters at that historic summit were full of respect, admiration and praises for him.

I must confess. I learnt a lot from him during this period. I was of course not surprised when he was posted to Geneva, where he equally excelled. Ambassador Anaedu left his footprints in the UN and other Multilateral Arena and I am sure many of his colleagues across the world, who worked with him in the UN and other Multilateral circuits, will also be saddened by his sudden demise. Certainly Ambassador Anaedu did a good job flying the flag of Nigeria across the World. Our dear 'Sita' ran a good race, fought a good fight and kept the faith. His memories will endure in our hearts and will have a place in the "Nigerian Foreign Service Hall of Fame" eventually.

"World Osy" – A Heartfelt Tribute
Ambassador Kayode Laro
Nigerian Ambassador to France and Monaco

Everyone seems to have a story to tell about Osy or *"World Osy"* as I called him. Our paths crossed back in 1984 shortly after we joined the MFA (Ministry of Foreign Affairs). But it was not so much within MFA because we were never in the same department; but in 1004 Flats, Victoria Island, where we both lived on Crescent C. Back then he was living with a mutual friend, an Information Officer, whom I had known from ABU (Ahmadu Bello University),

Zaria, where we both graduated in 1980. I would go to their apartment most evenings to hang out with them, to borrow an American expression. When our mutual friend got married outside Lagos, Osy and I and his younger brother, Jude, travelled there in the same vehicle. That was in 1985, if my memory serves me right.

Before long, Osy built a reputation as a hardworking officer. Again, if my memory serves me right, I think Osy as a 3rd secretary, worked without a problem under Ambassador Abuah, generally seen back then by young officers as a tough, terrifying boss.

From the late 80s, our paths didn't cross again until we met in Geneva in 2010 when I was posted there to "vice" him, to borrow MFA language. Ambassador Umunna Orjiakor came in the following year as Ambassador to Switzerland and Permanent Representative to the United Nations Office in Geneva and met Osy and me on the ground.

Before his arrival, Ambassador Charles Onianwa, a most perfect gentleman, was the Chargé d'Affaires. I have the warmest of memories from the time I worked under Ambassador Onianwa and Ambassador Orjiakor.

By the time I arrived in Geneva, Osy had become an expert in multilateral affairs, having worked at the Permanent Mission of Nigeria to the United Nations in New York. It was in New York that Osy established his reputation as an expert in climate issues to the extent that he would be independently invited to major UN conferences on climate.

But Osy didn't leave Geneva on my arrival as he got an extension to complete the work he was doing on the Human Rights Council as desk officer and head of the African Group's human rights experts. Back then, Western delegations and their allies had started their push to "mainstream" LBGT issues within the Human Rights Council but Nigeria and the African Group were resisting. And Osy led the charge on behalf of the Group. He provided strong leadership to his fellow experts in the group which was why, instead of serving a one-year term, he held the position of coordinator of the group for an unprecedented 3 consecutive years. The African Group simply saw no reason why they should replace him. That's how good Osy was at his job. Western delegates thought Osy was hard-charging and abrasive but he didn't let that bother him, knowing that he had the backing of the African Group.

On top of the work he did on the Human Rights Council, Osy was also the desk officer for WIPO (World Intellectual Property Organisation), one of the busiest schedules in Geneva. It takes a lot to be able to combine the Human Rights Council with WIPO as a desk officer.

From Geneva, Osy was sent to the PM-NY (Permanent Mission, New York), to work on the report of Nigeria's 2010-2011 tenure on the UNSC (United

Nations Security Council). As it turned out, the Australian candidate for WIPO DG in 2014, Francis Gurry, who won re-election to the post having been initially elected in 2008, appointed Osy as a special assistant. So Osy went from Geneva to NYC and back to Geneva. But he didn't meet me in Geneva on his return as I had been cross-posted to the PM-NY to work on the UN Security Council team as political coordinator under Ambassador (Prof) Joy Ogwu, who was the Nigerian Permanent Representative in NY at the time. I even ended up occupying Osy's former apartment in Tudor City, in Midtown Manhattan.

Osy went on secondment to WIPO and retired from there. He also got his *ambassador-in-situ* appointment while he was at WIPO. Absolutely well deserved, I must add.

We didn't see each other again until sometime in 2019 when we met at a workshop hosted by Amb. Martin Uhomoibhi at the head office of his think-tank PAIGAS. Ambassador Ibukun Olatidoye, Ambassador Abdul Aziz Dankano and Ambassador Okey Muoh were there too as resource persons just like me and Osy. As fate would have it, that was the last time I saw Osy, but thank God it was a cheerful reunion. We shook hands and hugged. Anyone who was close to Osy would know that he had an almost "trademarked" way of shaking hands. He would clasp your hand firmly and snap his fingers all in one move. I always got that special handshake whenever we met. Alas, I got it for the last time that day at PAI-GAS.

Rest in peace, nwannem, "World Osy". May God comfort the loved ones you left behind.

Utu Long, Mr Abrasive!
Ambassador Ndubuisi Amaku

Yes, "abrasive"! That is the word the West and others versed in *argumetum ad hominen* preferred to use when you deploy superior logic and argument in debates and discourses with them especially, when they feel their interest is threatened, or they are about to lose the argument. This was Osita's tactics in negotiations, which he characterised as the strategy of dominance and "dominate".

In one of Osita's major outing at *Yar'adua Centre* in Abuja, he lectured and lectured on how a negotiator can "dominate" in negotiations and leave one's opponent dazzled and sometimes weaker. This was one of his greatest assets. A consummate Multilateralist negotiator, Osita was a dominant and domineering negotiator with a prodigious intellect and a towering persona. Osy had not only a versatile talent but was also blessed with a fecund and fertile brain and imagination.

A diplomat's diplomat whose huge potentials veered and transcended into other fields of human endeavours which included, amongst others, wellness, human therapy for well-being and optimal living. Is it not an irony that his knowledge and skill could not save him?

Osita was most of the time concerned and preoccupied with advancing the welfare, goodness and happiness of others than for himself. That was why he was an astute builder of bridges in moments of hiccups and misunderstandings between friends, colleagues and neighbours. He brought me and Ambassador Abuah, the genius, closer after I had rebelled against what I considered high handedness, arbitrariness and an overreach by a boss.

Utu long, now that it is confirmed that you have passed on, what do I have to say again, to a dear friend, an authentic and committed brother like you but to conclude that you have validated the saying that good men die young. Osy, you were a good man and those who knew you will miss and forever mourn you. Farewell, *"Utu Long"*, Mr Brilliance, a consummate and tireless Negotiator, until we meet again to part no more.

Firm handshakes that radiated love and warmth
Ambassador Onijala

This is saddening. He was one of the very close officers to me. I did not see him recently. I did not know he was having health issues. His handshakes were firm and radiated love and warmth. His laughter spread love and his intelligence was illuminating. I recall the promotion exam we took in London at the

Mission in 2006. After the exam, we got into a bus to the hotel. Anaedu was very pensive and was not contributing to our discussions. Amb Uhomoibhi asked him why he was not his good self. He responded by saying that the questions so weakened him that he could not release his weapons of mass destruction! He was a good fellow. May he rest in peace. Amen!

A rebel against the word "impossible"!
Ambassador Umunna Orjiakor

This is sad, absolutely devastating. Osita worked with me in Geneva. He had a brilliant, voracious mind, inquisitive and bold. He was a hard-working officer, in other ways, a true force of nature.

Osita was possessed of a restless spirit that rebelled against the word "impossible", and he went out of his way to prove it. His magnum opus – *Your Microbiome* – is a testimony to the scope and versatility of his mind. His early death is also an irony that serves to revalidate what we already know – the power of God Almighty over everything. May his soul rest in peace, IJN. Amen.

Wondering what has become of Osy
Ambassador Ayalogu

Terrible news! Only a few days ago, I was wondering what had become of him as I wasn't hearing from him or anything about him, knowing him not the type to just fade into inertia or oblivion. He was full of life and full of great ideas and ideals.

He was particularly helpful to me when I was in Geneva and periodically visited New York on multi-lateral business.

His passing is clearly a major loss. May GOD Almighty receive and grant his soul eternal peaceful rest. Amen!

But what is Happening?
Ambassador Bassey Archibong

Oh my God. What is really happening? Within a space of one week, I have lost two office roommates i.e., late Amb. Rabiu Akawu and now Osy Anaedu. Four of us, Ambassadors Akawu, Olatunde, Anaedu and my good self, shared one room in Inter-African Affairs Department then under late Amb. A.D.J. Blankson and Amb. Ejor Abuah. Osy a fine officer and UN guru. Nigeria has lost a rare gem. Osy, my brother, please rest in perfect peace.

A peaceful, social and jovial gentleman
Ambassador Hassan. Mohammed

A peaceful, social and a jovial gentleman, full of lively laughter and energy. We launched his book on microbiomes on the 24/7/2021. He was so pleased with the success of the event that he promised to write another one which will touch on our time in New York, when we both served at the Permanent Mission. It is very sad that Osita is no more!

May his very gentle soul rest in perfect peace and may the Good Lord grant the family the fortitude to bear this great loss. I will miss this gentleman and a great diplomat by any measure! RIP, my friend.

Mr Anaedu I knew
Ambassador Taju Adeniyi

I fondly called him Anaedu when I was Personal Assistant to Ambassador Zubair Kazaure, DG (African Affairs) on the 6th Floor of 23 Marina. Ambassadors Anaedu and Isa Manaja worked closely as Third/ Second Secretaries under Ambassador Ejoor Abuah. As I was clearing house in Amb. Kazaure's Office, we of necessity had to interact. But after our Posting on Attachment in 1990, we never worked together again except to exchange pleasantries on the corridor.

Thanks to the Administration of President Olusegun Obasanjo that sold our apartments to us, we again became neighbours on 11th Crescent around 2005. He would stop over in my apartment, and we discussed about MFA briefly or about our infrastructure before we both at various times went on posting and he stayed back in Geneva. For long, we didn't meet again until we both boarded British Airways when I was returning on vacation from Abuja to London and he was going back to Geneva while he was on secondment to WIPO from where he retired and he didn't come back to his house in Kado Estate again.

The above was a summary of my interactions with Late Ambassador Osita Anaedu. May his soul rest in peace.

A Mann of God, A Man of Good, A Man of Supreme Kindness
Melchiade Bukuru

The passing of Ambassador Anaedu provoked a shockwave among his friends and colleagues. A Man of God, a Man of Good, a Man of supreme kindness, one of the greatest diplomats of our time, had left us in deep sorrow and grief. He has joined his Creator. His Ancestors. Despite his premature death, Ambassador Anaedu had completed his mission, that of spreading kindness to one's keens, that of building a just and fair world. Throughout his diplomatic career, this ultimate peace and sustainable development fighter left a great legacy that his children ought to pursue.

Rest in peace my friend. May God, the Almighty, continue to pour on you and your family eternal blessings.

Praying for more of Osy
Ambassador C. N. Umelo

It's so sad to learn of the sudden passage of our brother and colleague, Amb. Osita Anaedu. With all the beautiful encomiums showered upon his memory, none can underestimate the level of inspiration and impact his life had on friends and colleagues. We pray for more of his like in our profession and communities. My condolences to his wife and family he leaves behind. May his caring soul find eternal rest in the bosom of the Lord. Amen!

Praying for more of Osy
Ambassador C. N. Umelo

It's so sad to learn of the sudden passage of our brother and colleague, Amb. Osita Anaedu. With all the beautiful encomiums showered upon his memory, none can underestimate the level of inspiration and impact his life had on friends and colleagues. We pray for more of his like in our profession and communities. My condolences to his wife and family he leaves behind. May his caring soul find eternal rest in the bosom of the Lord. Amen!

To be appreciated while still alive!
Anonymous

After going through all the tributes posted so far, especially the one posted by Ambassador Amaku among others, the genuineness of all the outpouring sadness and love for the sudden demise of the dear Ambassador is palpable. The air of sadness over his final and definitive exit could simply be felt!

I began to think that one thing keeps missing in the life of the individual. And that one thing is the fact that the individual often times doesn't have the privilege and opportunity of hearing all the accolades, eulogies and sweet-nothings from colleagues, families and friends while still alive!! Amb. Osy should have been here to hear and witness first-hand all the heart-warming truths being told about him! I guess he would have beaten his chest and said: THANK GOODNESS FOR THE GRACE FOR AN EVENTFUL CAREER AND LIFE!

I believe no one is in doubt of the towering and sterling qualities which Ambassador Osy exuded and epitomized!

I am just wondering and thinking aloud that humanity would be better served if some sort of get-together is organized during which time deserving individuals are surprised and told in their faces how impactful their lives have been.

Adieu Ambassador Osy!

Good night!

Let your gentle and warm soul rest in the bosom of the Almighty!

But, this thing called death, where's your sting?

Ebubedike! Ebubedike!! Ebubedike!!!
Ambassador Segun Apata

Gone to rest! It's difficult to reconcile with and accept the reality of your 'disappearance' from our firmament. It's more difficult that I have suddenly been denied the opportunity of my salutation to and batter with the son of Anaedu – *Ebubedike!*

"Out, out, brief candle! Life's but a walking shadow, a poor player that struts and frets his hour upon the stage and then is heard no more---." Undoubtedly, yours was a short candle that burned briefly. But your flames were very bright.

Nigeria, nay Developing Countries and indeed the global community was fortunate to have you among the very versatile team at the Mission of Nigeria to the United Nations in New York as the world ushered in the new millennium in 2000. There was much anticipation and excitement across the globe of a new world that the new millennium portends for humanity. It was in this very historic period that Nigeria was elected by its peers in Developing Countries – about 133 of them, to lead and be the Chairman of our negotiating Group, the G77 and China. The import of the Chairmanship is that a Diplomat from the Nigerian Mission has to lead G77 in negotiations with other UN Groups, such as the EU, Japan, United States, Canada, Australia, Russia and Republic of Korea etc on all issues on the United Nations agenda, be it Social, Economic, Environment, Budget and Finance – essentially all matters under the purview of Second, Third, Fourth and Fifth Committees of the United Nations General Assembly. You were part of the Nigerian team to Second Committee dealing with Economic and Environmental matters among others. And Ebubedike, you were indeed a star among your peers.

The elaboration of various documents and negotiations of Resolutions on these issues were complex, challenging and robust. I was very delighted at how you and others from our Mission took on the task of ensuring the most beneficial outcomes for Developing Countries. It is appropriate to recall that the very robust manner you handled a key part of a particular Resolution led to a profound disagreement, which escalated into a threat from a colleague of yours from one of the Developed Countries. I did not share with you how I would handle the matter when you brought it to my attention. You were therefore surprised when a couple of days later, your colleague approached you and apologized.

You traversed the historic building of world peace and security as well as development by the East River in New York with enthusiasm, robustness, candour, grace and gravitas of a well-bred Diplomat. You equally traversed 828 Second Avenue, New York, with charisma, grace and humour. Our delegation meetings were always exciting as you brought a lot of humour to cheer up your colleagues. It was at 828 Second Ave, New York, that I christened you *Ebubedike* as your charisma had embedded in it graciousness.

How can Tunde and I could have imagined that when we spent time with you, Amaka and the young Anaedus in 2018 in Geneva that we would not have the privilege of your company and humour again! We are all now left with pleasant memories of the times we spent together. Those pleasant memories are the flames that will continue to brighten our hearts and be our solid anchor as we say **Bon Nuit.**

Ebubedike! Ebubedike!! Ebubedike!!! Osita, the Son of Anaedu and my dear *Aburo*, Rest in Perfect Peace!

Ambassador Ositadinama Anaedu: A Friend, Colleague and Brother
Ambassador Charles N. Onianwa (Ikukuoma Asaba) and Enyi. Mrs. Patricia N. Onianwa (Odoziaku Asaba)

Your Excellency and dear brother, Ambassador Ositadinma Anaedu; Okosisi; a quintessential Diplomat; the fearless one; very jovial, kindhearted, thorough, lovable, a shining example among his peers, colleagues and friends.

His Excellency, Ambassador Ositadinma Anaedu, was cut out for the Diplomatic service, and it was not a mere coincidence or accident of history. His passion and flair to join and rise to the highest position in the Nigerian Diplomatic Service was unstoppable. Armed with the perquisite university degree and a personality ladened with all the right traits of a budding diplomat, Ambassador Anaedu joined the Foreign Service and through dint of hard work, determination and dedication, he gradually rose to the enviable position of a Director. He was quick to learn and found out the importance of specialisation in the Diplomatic Service.

Like many others who towed the line of specialisation, Ositadinma joined the ranks of Multilateralists in the Diplomatic world. His Diplomatic postings took him to the two most important posts and main hubs of Multilateral Diplomacy in the world – New York, USA, and Geneva, Switzerland. It was his stay in New York and more especially his sojourn in Geneva, Switzerland, that brought our two families together. I was then posted to Geneva as Nigeria's Deputy Permanent Representative to the United Nations Office in Switzerland. Although I was Ositadinma's immediate supervising officer on his specialised Desks of Human Rights and the United Nations World Intellectual Property Organisation (UNWIPO), I was yet to master the rudiments of Multilateral Diplomacy.

Geneva is the busiest United Nations outpost in the World and Osita proved beyond reasonable doubt that he was one of the best Multilateralists to the envy of his colleagues and admiration of his foreign counterparts. The very bold but hilarious part played by Ositadinma at the centre stage of world diplomacy will remain memorable and will never go unmentioned here.

The year was July 2012 and was a gathering of world leaders, especially at the Foreign Ministerial level to discuss Human Rights issues. The then United Nations Secretary-General was chairing the event and the likes of then United States of America Secretary of State, Hilary Clinton, were there. I was then the Acting Permanent Representative to the United Nations and Osita was assisting me as Minister Plenipotentiary in charge of Human Rights Desk in the Nigerian Mission. Both of us represented Nigeria at the meeting. The vexed topic then was the controversial issue of same sex marriages and the rights of LGBTS, i.e. Lesbians and Gay Rights.

The UN Secretary General spoke in support of Lesbians and Gay Rights and so with many others, especially the South African Representative, whose actions betrayed his African colleagues as he shifted from the earlier position adopted by his African Group in Geneva. As a trained diplomat who believed in subtle diplomacy, I spoke against the issue of gay marriages and, with a flowery language, I also condemned the place of LGBTQ in the Nigerian Society. Incidentally, the issue had already been debated and outrightly condemned by both members of the Nigerian Senate and House of Representatives then. This stance of the National Assembly became more meaningful at that time. We already had a backing. I thought I had already stated Nigeria's position to the world body and had hardly sat down when my brother, adviser and teacher, Ositadinma, stood up and requested to speak. He looked at me, smiled and nodded (this was his usual and smartest way of getting an approval knowing fully well that it would never be). It then dawned on me that we were already heading for deep trouble. Ositadinma spoke vehe-mently condemning the stance of the U.N. Secretary-General and his supporters.

He pointed fingers at the South African Ambassa-dor who spoke earlier and called him by his first name, Jerry, asking him to inform the world body that he had now changed his name from Jerry to "Jerry Boy" (an obvious reference to the South Afri-can Ambassador's unwavering defence for Gay and Lesbian Rights). Ositadinma did not just stop there, he addressed the U.N. Secretary – General, then an Asian, and condemned his lesbian and gay rights stance. He also accused him of misleading the rest of the world, more so as his country's stance was con-trary to his vowed position. Nearly every delegation in the Great Hall stood up, clapped, urged Osita on. It then occurred to me that his next move was to stage a walkout encouraged by the overwhelming support he got from the African Group of Ambassa-dors, the Asians and some Latino countries. I per-suaded him not to do that, knowing the full conse-quences of our actions. He agreed, which to my greatest surprise was unlike Osita. This earned him my trust, admiration and respect. We became closer and would thoroughly discuss and agree on every is-sue that would be presented to the UN Body.

Of course, the story did not end there. Our then Minister of Foreign Affairs and the Permanent Sec-retary called in the evening while we were still at the office, informing Ositadinma and me that the South

African Ambassador and his British counterpart called to report our total disrespect for the U.N. Secretary General and the World Body. It became clearer to me that one has to be like the Ositas of this world to survive the rudiments of Multilateral Diplomacy. This I did and spoke unequivocally and with passion, defending our actions and standing up for what we sincerely believed in, diplomacy aside. The incident surprisingly died a natural death.

Ambassador Ositadinma Anaedu was one of the finest Nigerian Diplomatic Officers I have ever come across. He was just too good to be true and he loved his job and treated it with passion. His hard work, loyalty and passion did not go unnoticed. The Government of the Federal Republic of Nigeria deemed it fit to appoint him as an Ambassador Extraordinaire and Plenipotentiary, a position he held while working with the United Nations World Intellectual Property Organisation (UNWIPO) until his death. His Ambassadorial position became the crowning glory of his career in diplomacy. But then Osita's pillar of support came from his most beloved family. He married a wife who was also very bold, fortright, loving, loyal, caring and a great host to many. She fully understood her husband's passion for diplomacy and not only positioned herself for this great role ahead but supported him in everyway possible for a successful career.

His wife and children were his everything. He lived and worked tirelessly to ensure that they had the best things of life. Your Excellency, Mrs. Amaka Anaedu, thank you for being there for him always, especially at the last moments of his life.

Our dear friend and brother, Ositadinma, I and my spouse whom you always treated as a great sister, greet and bid you farewell. My children and grand-children also bid you farewell. You will never be for-gotten.

Adieu great one!!! May your gentle soul and those of all the faithful departed, through the mercy of God, rest in perfect peace. Amen!

Remembering Ambassador Ositadinma Anaedu.
Prof. Joy Ogwu

Our sense of loss at your untimely departure is in-describable. Indeed, we are still in disbelief that you have left this mortal plane.

No TRIBUTE or recollection could adequately express the depth of what you meant to so many. You had no guile, no pretensions, uniquely excep-tional, courageous, strong-willed, wise, yet respectful and modest. You were always at the foot of the Cross for others in all seasons. Your unwavering positivity was not only encouraging, but remarkably infectious. You always chose the way of truth, and never hesi-tated to face contentious issues in love and dignity.

Professionally, you deftly combined your encyclo-pedic knowledge, intellectual prowess and unswerving commitment with an enduring devotion to Nigeria's Foreign Service. I daresay we are all the richer for your indomitable spirit in pursuit of Nigeria's multilateralism.

May the Angels welcome you into God's presence. Your spirit ennobles us, and so does your legacy. Your legacy will find expression in the young family you have nurtured. May Amaka, the children, and extended family be comforted by the happy memories of your times together.

Picture Gallery

Osy, the UN Diplomat

U.N. HUMAN RIGHTS COUNCIL
OSITADINMA ANAEDU
Nigerian Permanent Representative to U.N. Office
in Geneva; Representing the African Group

C-SPAN
c-span.org

NEXT U.N. SECRETARY GENERAL BAN KI-MOON: SANCTIONS ON LIBYA 5:50am ET

Osy, the Family Man

Osy, Rosa and Ekwui

With Fada Onyii after priestly ordination, 19.08.1995

With Chdinma at her wedding, 02.03.2002

The whole family at Uju's wedding, 27.05.2000

With Chidi and her late husband, Pascal, at his wedding with
Amaka, 08.10.2005

Portrait of a happy couple, Amaka and Osy

Visiting with Fada Onyii in Grieskirchen, Austria, Easter 2006

Holding his son, Kamtoo, at the hospital after birth

Proud father with his daughter, Kosi

Queen Ann visiting with Osy and family in Geneva

With Fada Prof Ben Ejeh in Geneva

With Kosi at Heathrow Airport, UK

Visiting Kosi in school

Christmas holidays with his family in Austria, at the train station in Wels

Osy doing what he does best: being on stage and making speeches!

With Damian Ude (Dikegburugburu), his wife Nwaukay and
big sister Rose

With Fada Onyii and Brother Jude at Fada Onyii's covid-de-
layed silver jubilee celebration, 02.01.2022

At the wedding of his first niece, Gertrude Nnebụndo
Orakwue nee Ufo

With the in-laws, the Udeagbala family

With former Nigerian President, General Abdulsami Abuba-
kar and Bishop Matthew Hassan Kukah and other friends at
his home in Geneva

With Fr George Ehusani, Msgr. Obiora Ike and a friend

With Pat and Uju at a traditional marriage ceremony in the US,

With Uncle Arch. Emeka Aguluka and cousin Ositadinma Maduagwu and their wives

Osy was always current with the fashion of his time!

Ambassador Osy as a YouTuber

His magnum Opus, a 684-page book

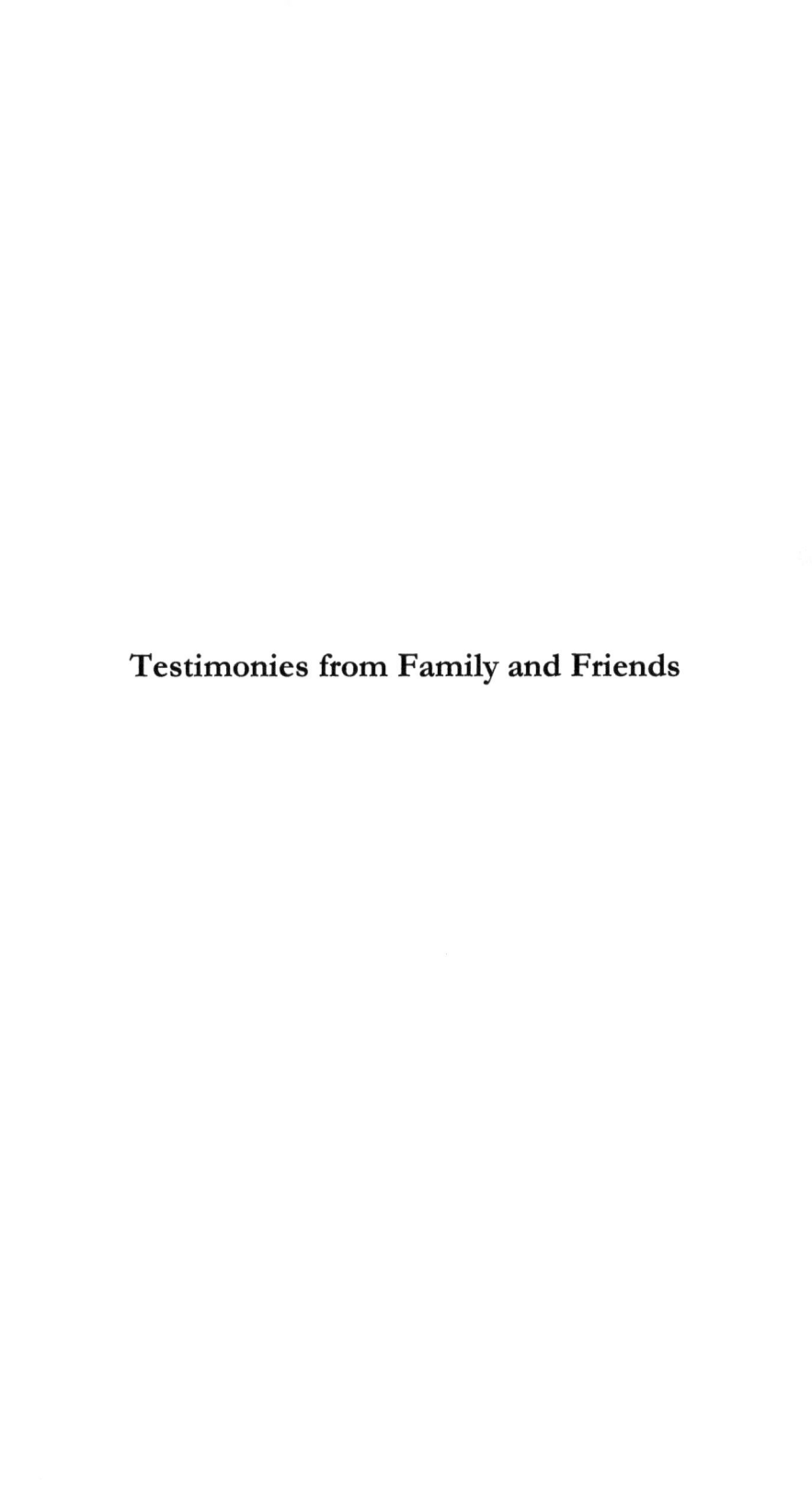

Testimonies from Family and Friends

Where Pain and Beauty Mingle – To my wonderful Babe and Daddy to my Children
Amaka Anaedu

Should I duck or not? That was the question as I waited at the arrival section of the local airport at Ikeja, Lagos, that day. Then I saw a familiar face – the resemblance was striking. As I made out from the corner where I was, there you were walking towards me determining this was the person you had come to meet.

That started a journey, which to some will be surprising and perhaps shocking. For 3 weeks from there, you were meeting my parents, another 3 weeks, we had our traditional wedding, and 3 months from there, we pledged our love before God and His church.

And what a journey it has been! The most precious and amazing gifts God gave us in our children, your tireless work day and night to see that we were ok and comfortable. I never regret saying 'Yes' to you. You were always there for me and our children. You were a strong pillar of support. I miss you badly. It wasn't always smooth sailing, but we were on top of it all until it pleased the good Lord to call you home.

Where do I even start? You were a role model to our kids, a strong pillar of support, and my sounding board – for you were a wise man. A consummate Diplomat, a Diplomat's Diplomat. An incredibly kind and compassionate human being with an unending sympathy towards others even when it was apparent that you were or have been hurt. Your patience was one of a kind. You gave chances upon chances and never gave up hope to which I always questioned you.

Many didn't know that considerations for our kid solidified the reason for our returning to Geneva from New York. I was worried because I felt you were giving up a lot, but you constantly maintained that you won't have it otherwise. Your child FIRST!

Nna m, chai! *Ọnwụamaegbu!* It wasn't supposed to be this way. You had dreams and plans for us and the children. Eleven days to your home calling, you were telling me of how you structured your plans after beating this monster of a disease. So what now? A good and dear friend of ours said to me *'God isn't finished with Osita, watch and see'*. I have hope. I know that our Redeemer liveth.

For those who knew you, you were one of a kind when it came to what you ate. After you successfully found a way to manage your health – your carry-on luggage was always filled with assorted medications and you diligently took all every morning before you stepped out of the house or anywhere – you gave up going for check-ups. We argued, but you always told me which I preferred: *You with all the medications you took or the one I see, healthy and strong!* I always caved in because you were right. You were never ill. I always joked that I was the one utilising the insurance we had, except for the kids' usual yearly control. You tried getting me on board with your healthy eating habit, but I couldn't cope. I often teased you as to what happened with your taste buds. However, you were successful with our children. They delighted in eating and drinking the special dishes and drinks you prepared. You took them out to road walks, running and exercising. This is where I hurt so badly because they clearly need them now, but I just can't keep up.

You took working to a whole new level. You would stay up the whole night writing, wake up and still go out the next day like nothing happened. I often teased you that if we had dated, I might not have married you because I realized that you were married first to your job. This caused me much grief because I asked myself what you got at the end. God knows and He will reward you adequately.

Baby, I'm not ok. Who will call me *Ugonwaanyi* again? Whom do I talk to? You did make some headway with me. I am not quick to respond as I usually did, you taught me to be patient in suffering. I think I am trying, and you always encouraged and appreciated the little steps I made.

We were a team in our marriage. You took care of paperwork and every other thing, while I handled all that pertains to the kids. Funny how every time you kept asking me for the children's birthdates, I told you but you would ask me again the next time. I just looked at you and we laughed.

Nna m, I dropped a tear in the ocean. The day you will find it is the day I will stop missing you. Like Mahatma Ghandi said: *There are no goodbyes for us. Wherever you are, you will always be in my heart".* For, you *may be physically absent, but your legacy lives on even in your absence.*

Goodnight my darling! Until the Resurrection morning! I love and miss you dearly.

My loving Dad
Kamtochukwu Anaedu

Dad, I wish I knew you better, because I know you but not as much as I would have liked to. I would have liked to have those father and son talks, that friendly banter. But I guess that will have to wait until after death.

Dad, he was a kind, amazing and caring person. He loved taking us out to exercise, and as a lot of you know, was very healthy and also gave us some of his drinks, and when we were sick (I and Kosi), they worked wonders!

He was always encouraging and happy when we got good results at school. We always talked together a little, Kosi, I and Dad, even when he was away. He was the perfect mixture of being nice and strict in the way that he wanted us to succeed. He was always interested in world politics and sports, and I learnt more because of him! I fondly remember actually, one day, we asked Mom if we could play video games, and she said no. After we asked Dad and he said yes! Then Mom came downstairs and wasn't happy when she saw us playing! She found out Dad said yes! Ever since then, he always told us to ask Mom if we asked to play video games. I remember too that when I was smaller, I asked Dad who he supported in football, and to my surprise, me, an ardent Manchester United fan, and still am, he said that he just liked good football. He was a tender man, but a lion in the art of diplomacy.

Dad, don't worry about us, we're okay and will be okay! Rest in peace! Love you!

To Daddy in Heaven
Kosisọchukwu Anaedu

I love you Daddy. I hope you are having a good time in heaven. I am sad that you went, but now, you can rest in peace eternally. Please watch over our family.

I love you

Our Hero is gone!
Rose Ufo, the big sister

My brother, Ambassador Ositadinma Anaedu, our hero is gone. Our darling brother! Your illness caught us unawares. When we heard that you were not well and you told us that you were getting better, we believed you and prayed that God would grant you quick recovery. Little did we know that this would lead to the end of your life.

Dear Osy, Ebubedike, we never knew that you would leave us so soon. We cherished our good days, when we stayed together chatting and hoping for a better future. But see how the cruel hand of death took you away from us. We cannot be with you anymore, you have gone home so soon.

How can we, your siblings, your wife and your children live without you? May Our Mother Mary, Our Mother of Perpetual Help, receive you in her mantle. And may the good Lord grant you eternal rest. Amen!

Adieu Ebubedike!

Good Bye Ambassador!

The Iroko tree has fallen!!
Queen Ann

When a great man died for years the light he leaves behind, lies on the path of men. – Henry Wadsworth Longfellow.

Ambassador Ositadinma Anaedu left his light in the path of men in the following ways:

1) He demonstrated a remarkable leadership qualities including advocacy of peace while serving his country, Nigeria, in the United Nations.

2) He had an electrifying presence with a smile that disarms even his enemies.

3) He lived a life characterised by a high level of forgiveness, a positive thinker, with an uncanny ability to see the bigger picture. A focused and goal-oriented man.

4) He goes over and beyond himself to achieve any target he set for himself.

5) He was a philanthropist who sponsored both local and international scholarships for students.

6) He was a great negotiator. His effort in negotiations helped him to draft, all by himself, the UN Resolution 55/188, which passed in one session. This resolution was a document, which enabled Nigeria to request for the return of illegally stolen money sent abroad.

7) He lived all his life for Nigeria and Africa, and they will indeed miss his contributions and negotiations in the United Nations.

Nevertheless, I'm still in denial that Ossy nwanne m, as I fondly called him, has gone. I'm still waiting to hear his voice calling Ann B (meaning the big Ann). He saw me as an all- rounder and a goal getter. He believed in me, even when I didn't believe in myself. He thought that I was a great designer, for when I design, the whole world copies.

I remembere, when I was going for my American visa. The moment his name was mentioned, doors and windows were opened and my visa was out. Travelling to America, I was the only black person in that particular air craft. I gave credit to God and Osy nwanne m. Reaching to America, Pat O Pat, husband to my baby sister, Ujunwa, took me round and we came to a place called World Trade Centre. He said to me, Ann O Ann, you see this building, terrorist are targeting it seriously. I screamed, wahoo!! So when it happened, I wasn't very surprised.

Ambassador nwanne m was a traveller. When he travelled, he carried along his loved ones. When I visited him in Geneva, it was fun. Osy was a good Christian, married to Amaka and had with two boisterous children, Kamtoo and Kosi.

Ambassador, my sweet brother, you lived an exemplary life until your triumphant transition to heaven, may your guardian angel lead you to the bosom of our Lor Amen!

Adieu nwannem nke m

Ebubedike of Igboland!!

Okenwa, (the golden child)

The entire family will miss you so dearly we pray that God our good Lord will grant you a peaceful resting place and us the fortitude to bear this irreplaceable loss.

My Brother, Osita, Man of of Character!
Jude Anaedu

In a world that is filled with darkness, you were able to bring a light shining through the darkness to lead people to success and to God. You embodied the light of Christ when you shared His love with others as Jesus did, serving them with peaceful hearts and directing them toward God's provision and mercy. You touched the lives of everyone around you. You encouraged the people to live in accordance with hard work, perseverance and in God. You lived a life that gave hope to those around you.

The world is full of darkness and people like you help to bring light shining through the darkness, hope and joy to others. You did this by sharing love with others, serving them with peaceful hearts and directing them towards achieving success or feeling helped.

Your charity works are well noted and you did it all without asking for anything in return. This is why I say a man's character is his fate. Heraclitus Thomas Jefferson, the third President of the United States (US), said: *"Nothing can stop the man with the right mental attitude from achieving his goal; nothing on earth can help the man with the wrong mental attitude."* Nothing was able to stop you and your character was actually your light, which shone for all to see.

British writer and politician, Thomas Macaulay (1800-1859), said: *"The measure of a man's character is what he would do if he knew he never would be found out."* I have often said that what would ultimately destroy a man going to high places in life is not really the enemies that are waiting for him there, but the character that followed him there. Your character took you to the topmost height of your career, which you performed excellently.

To build relationship, you said one must learn to treat people with courtesy. The Shunammite woman in the Bible is an example. She must have been praying for a child all through her life. By being hospitable to a man of God, she eventually got her much-awaited miracle. It wasn't just her prayer that opened the door for her; it was her character. Assuming she wasn't hospitable, she would have missed a critical miracle.

Many times, we pray, fast and bind demons that don't exist when our real demons are just our greatly flawed characters. Many have insulted people that were divinely placed and orchestrated to help them fulfil their destiny. Some people are keeping malice with their destiny helpers.

Treat people with respect.
Treat strangers with courtesy.
Never look down on anybody. God can use anyone to change your story.

Abigail Van Buren said: *"The best index to a person's character is how he treats people who can't do him any good, and how he treats people who can't fight back."* You can easily judge the character of a man by how he treats those who can do nothing for him. The way we treat people we think can't help or hurt us like housekeepers, waiters, and secretaries, tells more about our character than how we treat people we think are important. I know you treat those with so much love and respect. I have seen on occasions interacting with them. Now I want show you two good examples I could find of importance of GOOD CHARACTER.

When the ancient Chinese decided to live in peace, they made the Great Wall of China; they thought no one could climb it due to its height. During the first 100 years of its existence, the Chinese were invaded three times and every time, the hordes of enemy infantry had no need of penetrating or climbing over the wall, because each time, they bribed the guards and came through the doors. The Chinese built the wall, but forgot the character-building of the wall-guards. Though the Great Wall has over the years become a powerful symbol of the country's enduring strength and spirit, it has actually been a good reminder to the Chinese of the superiority of human character. How many people and homes had been invaded, looted and devasted by the enemy through the bribery of ego, self-indulgence, insincerity and unfaithfulness. The scriptures say *"while men slept, the enemy came and sow tares into the harvest and go their way"*.

The Chinese realised much later that the best defence against the enemy is not a fortified wall, but a fortified character. Thus, the building of human character comes before the building of anything else. This is why it is normally said that a man without character is unstable and cannot be trusted.

Be mindful of your words and how you speak to people. This shows what you have within you. Work seriously on your character and attitude towards life. This was often your kind of advice to others. Peter Schutz, the former chief executive officer of Porsche said: "HIRE CHARACTER; TRAIN SKILLS."

Secondly, in the days when Germany was divided, a huge wall separated East and West Berlin. One day, some people in East Berlin took a truck load of garbage and dumped it on the West Berlin side. The people of West Berlin could have done the same thing, but they didn't. Instead they took a truck load of canned foods, bread, milk and other provisions, and neatly stacked it on the East Berlin side. On top of this stack they placed the sign: *"EACH GIVES WHAT HE HAS"*.

Osita, my brother, you were a man of integrity. In other words, you accept the risks that come with being consistent and true to your own values in every situation. You are always willing to make the right choice rather than the easy choice. You didn't have to make excuses. You always stuck with the truth even if the truth makes you look bad.

May your soul rest in peace. Amen. Farewell my brother. We all love you and miss you.

My Gracious Brother is Gone!!!
Lady Eucharia Udeh, LSM

I have been in denial. He is sleeping and will soon wake up. I waited patiently to get my usual call of *"Nwaukay, how are you doing today?"* since that black Sunday to no avail. Behold, IROKO nwannem has fallen. Ebubedike ndi Igbo has slept on. The sun has eclipsed. And Nigeria just lost a seasoned career diplomat. Africa indeed will miss your contributions and negotiations in the United Nations.

You towered and bestrode your paths like a colossus. You shone like a billion stars. Your charm was very charismatic and yet very humble. You were a fighter! The resolutions you sponsored at the UN are what many African nations are benefiting from today.

An eloquent speaker and astute negotiator, who came up with a draft for the return of illegally stolen funds to the countries of origin. With powerful lobbying, you were able to have that drafted resolution passed in ONE SESSION – a feat that Nigeria had never achieved before and ever since. That resolution – UN Resolution 55/188 is the foundational document that enables Nigeria and other developing countries to request the return of illegally stashed loot, which led to the return of billions of dollars to Nigeria from multiple countries.

Ambassador Ositadinma Anaedu was a great man! According to Robert Green Ingersoll, *"A great man does not seek applause or place; he seeks for truth; he seeks for the road to happiness and what he ascertains, he gives to others"*. Very typical of who you were – selfless. But Nigeria would rather reward politicians who are the benefactors of the returned loots with MON.

Our mother of great memories used to tell us stories depending on what she wanted to share and teach us. She usually does that after dinner – the secret of the bonding and the laughter in our family. We took turns to tell stories and discussed the morals of each story and folklore. I noticed that Ambassador's stories never ended. One story can last for one month or more. Once it was his turn, he would continue with the story and embellish it with different moral codes, with teasers that would make us laugh our heads odd and he always had Chidinma as his accomplice.

Not until I grew up that I realised that his stories were intentional, targeted to making us better human beings. Sister Ann would always ask him *this your story o na-agwukwa agwu?* (*This your story never ends?*). He would reply that *palmwine could never finish in the house of palmwine tapper.* The difference between his stories and Mama's stories was that, while mama did her own after dinner, his own was anytime there was an opportunity, so he was naturally a teacher. With that he commanded loyalty and respect. In furtherance, he created bonding in the family.

Osy had a way with words and phrases that beautifies his statements and arguments and I loved listening to him. It was big fun eavesdropping to him and his friends discussing topical issues on politics, football, girls, etc, with the likes of Air Commodore Chukwma Adogu, Senator Victor Umeh, Misaro Walter Adogu, Vincent Ezewuzie, pretty Baby *be* Achalu, Ann B Nebechianya, Mary and Pauline Ibeneme, Maurice Anaetoo, Bartholomew Anaetoo, Inno Maduagwu, Dr Ogbukili, Iwoliwo, etc. I would usually slide myself into a vintage corner ready to serve them from mama's generous pots with Chidinma. All my siblings enjoyed their conversations, which increased our vocabulary and learning. Indeed, it was awesome. So beautiful as in listening to Rev Fr Emmanuel Umezinwa talk and sing in his FM radio programme: *Music from the Masters!*

My brother was a giver, a great giver with a large heart. A chip of the old block, he carried this grave of giving from our father and mother. Our parents were great philanthropists. And Ambassador took it to another level, becoming a giver of knowledge, love, scholarships, other charity projects etc. He had no limits. His house was wide open to accommodate people, even his enemies. A confident man who was not afraid of putting people in the position greater than his own. Rare breed of leadership as *"eze afọ juru"* (*a king full of satisfaction*). Sometimes he felt frustrated by ingrates, who repay goodness with evil, but it never ever deterred him to continue helping.

Osy was very lovable and kind. He had pet names for the girls:

> Sr Rose is *sister me*
> Sr Ann is *Ann B*
>I am *Nwaukay*
>Chidinma is *Achidibabe*
>Uju is *Prettie*
>Late Ekwy is *Okwie*

My dear brother fare thee well. To say we will miss you is an understatement. But we take consolation in your encounter with the priest that gave you viaticum, had your confessions and gave you the Blessed Sacrament. Immediately he concluded these rites, he had a gentle voice of God say to him: *"HE IS A GRACIOUS MAN, BUT WILL NOT MAKE IT"*. What else can we ask for when you are in heaven with your maker? Resurrection day awaits when we shall meet to part no more.

My love, bye bye.

Ezigbo nwanne nọ dị mma....

He called me "ACHIDINMA"
Chidinma Oduchukwu

Brother mee! That's what l fondly call you. My dearest brother, Amb. Osita Anaedu (Ebubedike Igbo), your demise was like a film to me because we spoke every day during your brief illness not knowing God's time for you is now but the whole thing dawned on me after one month I have not heard that name you call me "ACHIDINMA".

Brother mee, I will not mourn you, but I prefer to celebrate you for your short but eventful sojourn in life and your passionate career as an astute diplomat. All your colleagues, friends, relatives, well-wishers, in fact, anybody that had one thing or the other to do with you are all testifying how sincere, professional, trustworthy, loving, caring and reliable you were. I feel so proud to have had you as a brother.

Though you left so soon, I am consoled that God welcomed you into heaven.

JEE NKE ỌMA till we meet again to part no more!

He used to call me *Ụkọchukwu Ebeebe* (Priest forever)!
Fada Onyii

And I used to call him, "*Broda mii!*" with the sweetest of admiration and respect. Being nearly 13 years older than me, he was always the big brother I looked up to and admired. And being the one person I resembled most in physical appearance in our family, I

74

enjoyed a special bond with him, which my being a priest further cemented.

Osy always knew my apathy to longing for leadership and an unnecessary seeking of attention, a trait I must have inherited from my father in contradistinction to my mother, who was a born leader. Hence, he once said to me, when I was still in my teens as a junior seminarian: *"If good people avoid leadership positions, bad people will continue occupying them. Even though you people don't call it politics in the Church, the fact is that if good priests refuse to be in leadership positions in the Church in the name of humility and modesty, bad priests will be in those positions, and bet me, the Church will be worse for it."* This was how he introduced me to the bestseller at that time: *In God's name* by David Yallop, which he gave me to read. And having read this book at the age of 17, just immediately after my secondary school certificate examinations, my young and adolescent mind was equipped to deal with the scandals in the Church as they came and still keep coming.

I might not be as intelligent and as eloquent as Osy was. However, I think that, in my admiration of him and in my effort to emulate him, I inherited a little bit of both. While he pontificated with eloquence and brilliance at the UN sessions, the Church's pulpit became my comfort zone, where I often cannot explain how unprepared and spontaneous thoughts are delivered with such power of conviction that could only have come about through divine inspiration, occasionally moving the congregations into instinctive applause. Consequently, it was not just a happenstance that, while he was publishing his opus magnum on health, *Your Microbiome (Bacteria) is a Wonder of Nature: Activate and Optimize – Eating for Healthy Longevity* in 2020, I was putting finishing touches to my semi-autobiography in commemoration of my silver jubilee priestly anniversary (1995-2020): *Reminiscences of an Accidental Missionary*, published in 2021. And we had plans to jointly publish a work on his 'miraculous' cancer recovery because the effect of the treatment he was getting was nothing short of miraculous, until it took the unexpected negative turn. And we had many other plans together. But, as the saying goes: *man proposes, but God disposes!*

Yeah, my relationship with Brother Osy was such that anyone I introduced to him as my friend became, not just his friend too but part of the Anaedu family. My priest-friends, Reverend Sister-friends and lay friends, who all had the opportunity of having personal encounters with him, can all testify to this. And he kept contact with nearly all of them. How he did it? I don't know.

It will be an understatement to say that Brother Osy will be missed by me and by many, who knew him. But we have the assurance of our faith that he did not live in vain because ultimately, his death is gain.

Adieu *Broda mii!* Jee nke ọma!

Adieu, My Stepfather
Obianuju Okpala

Whenever I think about my brother, my step-father, I remember his bright smile. He had one for everybody he met along the way. I cry and cry, knowing that I will never be able to see that smile again.

The pain of his death is not something that can go away with just sincere condolences or a bunch of flowers. He left us a part of him that neither time nor even his death can ever take away. When I expressed my dream of going to college, he dreamt with me all the way to the United States of America.

He was loud and proud when I started my journey with him as a new graduate. Together with the whole family, he was with me every step of the way. Losing him is like losing my wings. Flying is close to impossible because the pain has crippled me. What keeps me going is that I would be wasting our dream if I stopped flying because I have lost him. He would want me to continue chasing my dreams bravely as if he was here.

He was not a saint, but he was the home that we could always return to because we knew that he would welcome us with arms wide open. We can all picture him with his signature smile telling us that he had got our backs.

As I think of the crowd of people mourning for him, I find comfort in knowing that all of you love my brother. I find peace in knowing that he touched your life and that you also touched his heart at some point in his life. I find happiness in knowing that he will live on in all of your memories. He may not have lived a perfect life, but he lived a good one. One that we will forever cherish and we will continue to re-member.

I know my brother would hate to see us crying for him. He would want us to cling to the beautiful mem-ories and forgive ourselves for whatever regrets we have. He would like us to be strong through the dark-est days ahead. That is what he always does – he gives light and strength when it seems impossible to go on.

I can never deny the pain that I carry, but I would like us to remember him as a blessing and a lesson. I want to treasure the life he shared with us over the pain that his death has brought us.

Rest in eternal peace, dear brother, stepfather, Ebubedike – The great orator and negotiator of our time!

My Great Uncle
Ngozi Ufo

I grew up knowing that I had a great man in my uncle. He was exemplary in everything he did, from academics to politics, at home, amongst his kinsmen, and at the United Nations center-stage, where he served. Uncle Osy, you loved greatly and sacrificed so much for the family you admired so much, the Paulinus Anaedu dynasty.

Growing up was so much fun. I remember all the good times we had at Onitsha, Agụlụzigbo, and in Lagos with you, Mama, Papa, my mum, Rosa, Aunty Ekwy of blessed memory, Aunty Ann, Uncle Jude, Aunty Eucharia, my second mummy, Aunty Chidex, Fada Onyii, Ujunwa, the love of the family, plus other grandchildren and the in-laws.

A big vacuum has been created in our hearts. Uncle Osy, who would make us smile, and made our hearts swell with pride when you stood up to address the crowd, be it at the local parish church in St Patrick's, Agụlụzigbo, or the *ụmụnna* meeting, or at the world's highest stages in the UN!

You were a great son, the son of your father, the late Paulinus Ọnwụzuligbo Anaedu, my grandfather. You fitted into the big shoes he left behind. He must have been very proud of you and all your achievements.

My very own hero! It was so hard watching you in pain in those last moments of your life. You fought as you always did at every stage of your life, so you could stay longer for us. I'm grateful to God for the privilege of serving and taking care of you on your sick bed. It allowed me to return my love and to take care of you as a daughter would do to a loving dad. Our hearts are broken because we would not see you again, but we are not left without hope. Our consolation is that you are resting in God's bosom. The

Lord gives and He has taken, and our souls are at peace with that.

I learnt the love for the family from you, it was very important to you. You taught me how to have passion in everything I do and to be the best I can be. You educated me on how to always raise my head high and be a good ambassador for my family and the society.

I learnt the essence of looking good always from you! What didn't you teach me when I came to live in Abuja with you for my internship program? You pushed me to come out of my comfort zone and face the world.

You were always full of praise for every little effort one makes, even as you corrected in love and encouragement. You touched many lives. You cared about everyone in your life no matter how low they were, and you never discriminated against them. On your sick bed, you had "strangers", whose lives you must have touched greatly, take care of you with such tender love.

I must not fail to show my admiration, appreciation, respect, and honor to Amb. Ejinaka, your bosom friend, Henry, David your driver, and little David for taking good care of you when we were not there.

Adieu my great and loving Uncle Osy!

Adieu my hero!

Adieu Ambassador Ositadinma Anaedu!

Adieu Ebubedike of Agụlụzigbo, until we meet again!

Just hard to believe!
Dr. Mrs. Gertrude Orakwue

Uncle Osy! I can hardly believe I'm writing your eulogy. You have been a blessing to me and our family. From when you were a young, single man, you had been all about family. Your house was a rallying point for us all.

As a teenager, your place was my go-to for vacations and holiday jobs. Your place was open to us all. I can't begin to express enough on the impact you had on me growing up. You made us all want to aim high and excel because you excelled in most of your endeavours. You were a man of high achievement and you tried to instil it in us. You would ask about my plans and advise. You were such a blessing and very generous too.

I remember my university days, when you would have pocket money for going back to school. You were the man with a big heart, a generous giver, an encourager! You always knew the most endearing words to say to cheer one up.

In recent times when we talked, you would always advise me on healthy living, being fit, being active etc. You were such a health champion. You even wrote a book on healthy living.

I remember our last conversation, when we talked of your healing. But alas, God had a better plan for you. May His name be praised!

Uncle, you ran your race and finished your course. We will miss you. Your transition is such a huge loss to our family.

Adieu my darling uncle, adieu *nwoke bụ sọ mma*!

To My Great Uncle
Chioma Nnolim

Ambassador Ositadinma Anaedu, Ebubedike! It is so hard to believe that you are truly gone. It was difficult to put myself together to write this tribute. It is so painful and devastating. I am still in denial I am still in shock. I wish I was having a bad dream.

When I heard about your sickness, I kept praying for you that you get better. Only God knows why you have to leave this world so soon. We loved you so dearly but it seems God loves you more. I pray by the grace of God that you are resting peacefully with no pains and sorrows with God in heaven.

Your death reaffirms our Catechism teaching that God made us to know him, to love him, and to serve him in this world and to be happy with him forever in the next. It also proves that our life on earth is so temporary. We all need to aspire by the grace of God to be with God in heaven after our journey in this life.

Uncle Osy, you made a very huge impact on our lives like a father. You worked really hard to attain your dreams and goals, being an Ambassador and all the wonderful things you did in this world. You always inspired us with your fatherly advice, moral, financial support and generosity. You set up very high standards for us to always look upon, to work hard and aim to be the best in whatever we do by the grace of God.

Oh! Uncle Osy, we will greatly miss you but your legacy, sweet memories and good deeds will live on in our hearts. We pray we will meet again in heaven to part no more.

God, please give us, your wife, your children and all of us the grace and fortitude to bear this irreparable loss.

I believe by the grace of God that your soul is resting in the bosom of our Lord Jesus Christ and covered under the mantle of our Mother Mary. May your gentle soul continue to Rest In Peace! Requiescat in pace!

Adieu, my very dear Uncle Osy, Ebubedike!

The Uncle, who knew me before I knew myself
Engr Emeka Ufo

My Uncle Osy was a great guy, no airs. Humble, hardworking, clever, creative, ingenious and very handsome. He knew me even before I knew myself. He lifted me to a different platform and I hit the ground running. The Anaedu family has lost a very special person. So many unfinished dreams and plans we had together. You left too soon. Nobody expected this, Uncle. Your mates are still strong and about but God knows the best.

I was in a train that cold December morning when I was told that you had died. I sobbed quietly in open glare of others. I was unashamed. It was a special gift to have known you and spent those times with you. You will be missed terribly. Thank you and thank God for you.

You went about doing good
Comas Ufo, brother-in-law

The news of your death was spine chilling. You were really a hero, having attained the best version of yourself. You were among the best people that Nigeria produced. Hence an ambassador, a man authorized to represent Nigeria in any country.

You went about doing good. So many people were able to be educated because you financed their education. Nobody in difficulty ever came to you without you giving the person assistance.

The remembrance of your departure keeps the tears ever flowing from our eyes. We pray that the Lord grant you eternal rest. Assured of the maternal solicitude of our Mother of Perpetual Help, you will reach heaven. I miss you, we miss you.

May God give us the fortitude to bear the loss.

Good bye Ambassador.

His Excellency, Ositadinma Anaedu, The People's Ambassador
Chief Patrick Okpala (Obisaambala)

Ambassador Osy Anaedu, was all anyone would have wanted in a man, husband, friend or colleague. He was a gentleman with an unmatched work ethic, an astute diplomat, a God-fearing man, a loving father and husband. I am privileged to be his in-law.

I met my wife, Uju, in his home in New York. It was unique how he walked a fine line between Igbo traditional values and American social demands in guarding and guiding Uju through our dating years to the D-day. He brought my wife to the United States right after her Undergraduate Studies in Nigeria. We are grateful. All through the years, Ambassador Osy was a father to many, especially to my loving wife. He was adored by our children. His constant calls and advice to our children were immeasurable ....advice on the right choices in life, their choice of universities, on social skills, on the need to imbibe our cultural values in their daily lives, etc. We miss and will forever miss those.

I am amazed by Ambassador Osy Anaedu's work, exercise and diet ethics. All he needed was an hour of sleep, and he will work through the night and arrive at his office bright and early. I have never seen a man do 400 pushups but he always did. His diet routine was regimented into value-added portions. I saw a super human being in my brother-in-law. Really heaven must have needed an angel. Ambassador Osy Anaedu was not supposed to die. Especially now. But I bow to the Lord's ordained destiny.

My wife, Uju, the Anaedus and the Diplomatic Community where he worked, know ye that *The People's Ambassador* was here on a mission, delivering life-saving benefits through the instruments of the United Nations, touching lives through his YouTube channels, educating the world through his Book Series and spreading love through his interpersonal relationships. Let us rejoice in his achievements and celebrate them. As we mourn, let us thank God for the opportunity of sharing this world with this beautiful soul, *The People's Ambassador*, Ositadimma Anaedu. Farewell my friend.

Adeiu, Rock of Anaedu Dynasty
Chief Barr/Lady Matthew and Caronline Udeh, KSJI

We celebrate the passage to the eternal glory of Ambassador Osy Anaedu, the rock of the surviving Anaedu family, and the eldest brother of our daughter-in-law, Lady Eucharia Udeh, nee Anaedu, who is married to my first son, Sir. Damian.

I pay him tributes, not only on behalf of my nuclear family, the Udeagbala Family of Umuome, Inyi, in Oji River Local Government Area of Enugu State, but also on behalf of the Association of Retired Biafra War-affected Police Officers from South East and South-South States of Nigeria, ARWAPO, whose delegation I led in 1995 to plead for the payment of retiring benefits to our members. Late Ambassador Osy Anaedu happened to be in Abuja at the relevant period and he played a liaison role by connecting us with the then Chairman of the Police Service Commission, who granted us the audience, which ultimately resulted in the approval for the payment of retiring benefits to our members who served in Biafra and were first dismissed at the end of the civil war, and later retired by Presidential Amnesty.

We pray to Almighty God to receive Osy's soul in His bosom and grant him eternal rest. Amen!

Ebubedike, an Embodiment of Cerebral and Emotional Intelligence!
Barr, Sir. Damian Udeh, KSM, Gburugburu Ikezuagu Kingdom, Brother-in Law

Agụlụzigbo shut down on the 2nd of January 2022, when Rev. Fr Onyekwelu Paulinus Anaedu – Fada Onyii (my brother-in-law) celebrated the Silver Jubilee anniversary of his priesthood. The entire Anaedu dynasty was in attendance and it was a grandiose occasion. Ebubedike was at his best on that day, dressed in his well-fitted ash-colored, senator-styled caftan. Everyone knows that he was a man of style and elegance and he shone brightly like a thousand stars on that day. He was everywhere, welcoming guests, directing activities, making speeches (for that was his specialty), regaling the guests with his usual qualitative, gold-standard deliveries filled with *'inu ndi igbo'* (Igbo proverbs) etc. That event came and passed and everybody returned to their workstations across the nation and the world. That was the last time I saw Ebubedike alive.

Darkness enveloped the land even in the daytime as news filtered in on that fateful 11th December 2022 morning, that Ebubedike, nwanne m, from another mother, the great sage and lover of all good things, exponential Ambassador, has passed on to the great beyond.

Ebubedike was indeed a total man, who has been through different experiences in life and does not let those experiences limit or define him. Anyone, who knew him, will admit that he was an embodiment of cerebral intelligence with an additional dose of emotional intelligence, qualities which had guided him through his very exemplary and meritorious career as a diplomat, serving Nigeria in many capacities across many countries of the world, and terminating at the Permanent Mission Office of Nigeria at the United Nations in Geneva. He listens and respects people's opinions and has a great sense of humor. Osy was empathic and shared your successes and your failures, standing tall to encourage you robustly in any good enterprise you may be involved in; he was a good family man and you will readily see this in the cohesion and fraternity that exist between him and his direct siblings, including my lovely wife, and most importantly the love that exists in his immediate family comprising his wife and kids.

It is a fact that nothing ever truly prepares one for the sudden demise of a loved one, especially when they are still in their prime and people are looking forward to the person's next milestone in life's journey. I however counsel that, even as we mourn, we should find solace in the fond memories of his life and times, the fact that he impacted many in the extraordinarily eventful life he lived, his contributions to bringing to the fore a better understanding of the field of alternative medicine and his immeasurable impact on the overall recognition of Nigeria as a country with great promise at the United Nations. I exit with the following poem which I direct to his lovely Amaka, Kamto, Kosi, Rose, Ann, Jude, Eucharia, Chidinma, Fada Onyii, and Ujunwa

You can shed tears that he is gone, or you can smile because he has lived.

You can close your eyes and pray that he will come back, or you can open your eyes and see all that he has left.

Your heart can be empty because you can't see him, or you can be full of the love that you shared.

You can remember him and only that he is gone, or you can cherish his memory and let it live on.

You can cry and close your mind, be empty, and turn your back, or you can do what he would want: smile, open your eyes, love, and go on.

Go well, gentle spirit, until we meet to part no more. Amen!

Osy, my Childhood-Friend and Brother
Commodore Chukwuma Adogu (Rtd)

Today, life has thrust on me the tough duty to write a funeral tribute to a bosom friend that was more of a brother, Ambassador Ositadinma Anaedu. Ours was a relationship that started right from our teenage days, running unbroken through adolescence on to adult life, sharing very close, deep and cherished moments.

It is such a difficult task to write this, not for want of what to say but because there is so much to write about the life and times we shared, beginning from the early 70s of the last century when we first met in one of the numerous parties secondary school students from our hometown, Agụlụzigbo, organised during holidays. Such gatherings were usually in make-shift halls of primary schools either in Oye or Akpu, but Osy graciously volunteered his father's compound for subsequent editions, and hosted quite a good number even on to our university days. It was such a close knit circle of bold, and yet decent teenagers in secondary schools, who were full of confidence for the future. Osy was one of the key drivers. Being senior to some of us in the pack, I admired and looked up to him as a role model. The bonding we achieved in those formative days laid the foundation for the very close relationship we enjoyed, subsequently.

Osy and I got further opportunities for closer interactions as providence kept throwing us together in same location virtually at every stage of life. I recall very many cherished moments starting from when he joined me first in Dennis Memorial Grammar School (DMGS), Onitsha, for his Higher School while I was in Class 5, then at the University of Nigeria, Nsukka, and later when he came for his NYSC in Kaduna, where I worked before joining the Nigerian Navy. We were later to practically live together at the 1004 Flats in Victoria Island, Lagos, before requirements of our military and diplomatic careers began to throw us to far-flung locations locally and internationally.

Osy was full of life, energetic, humorous, passionate, compassionate and particularly upright. All these qualities he brought to bear immensely in his career as a diplomat. Little wonder he made such a huge success of it and got to the pinnacle of his chosen career.

Death throws a whole new meaning when it happens to somebody we have associated very closely with, and have high regards for. It continues to shock us into grief despite knowing that its occurrence is inevitably tied to our very existence and nobody has control over when and how it will occur.

Osilentis (as I fondly called you), we had a beautiful childhood, a great youth and successful careers. We were looking forward to a splendid retirement, when we would have been done with all the achievements and return to a glorious old age in Agụlụzigbo. Little did we know that God had other plans to make you the fore-runner for us in Heaven.

Osilentis, we will miss you so dearly, your departure diminishes all of us that know you closely especially our small peer group of home boys. The gap it leaves in our being will ache for a long time and may never be filled. But who are we to complain when it pleases our Maker to call you home now?

Coming to terms with the finality of your death will indeed be a huge struggle. The solace we have is that you lived a good life, touching so many other lives positively.

We can shed tears that you are gone, and we do, but we can also smile because you lived and touched our lives...
We can close our eyes and pray that you come back or we can open our eyes and see all that you have left.
Our heart may be empty because we cannot see you again; or we can be full of the love and friendship we shared, and cherish the sweet memories and let them live on.

Death is the fate that awaits all mortals; your passing once more reminds us of this reality and offers us the chance once more for deeper introspection that would enable us moderate our lives appropriately while we still can.

Good night my dearly beloved brother, and fair winds as you soar in the firmament to journey back to your Maker.

My Iroko has been cut down
Emmanuel Sunday Ozoemena

I stepped into Chong King Mansion elevator in February of 1992, a lone man in an overcrowded Hong Kong, a city colony I had only read about in novels and only landed in a few days before. As the elevator climbed up, I looked around and noticed a face I thought was familiar. *How could that be?* I knew no one in Hong Kong. Or so I thought.

Then I thought quick and fast. I had met this man a few months earlier in Nigeria. In Onitsha. The shy me wanted to walk away as usual. But no, if this guy is who I was imagining – a brother to one of my best and most respected friends, then I would rue me thereafter. So I made my bold move:

"I am Onyii's friend from school... You are his senior brother Osy?"

"Yes" he answered, and the introduction went further and ended with him offering me his card and some cash for lunch.

Two days later I called him from Tokyo when in a difficult situation, a day after arrival. His suggestions and ideas got me through one of the most difficult days in my life.

Three years later we linked up in Nigeria and Osy became a senior brother to me too, discussing everything and offering advice. When my wife and I got involved in a serious car accident, Osy visited us in hospital every day before or after work.

Later in New York, while on a business trip a few weeks after 9/11, I stayed in his house and he accommodated me and my friend for almost a week and took us around town showing us places. .

An ambassador first-class, Osy travelled the world as he worked for our country, Nigeria, where he became an expert negotiator and our country's first voice within the Non-Aligned countries. At the United Nations, his zeal and expertise have shone for years as he carried our country's torch and flag in solving humanity's problems and doing the complex negotiations involved.

Even before I met you, conversations with Onyii about you helped steer my interests to international relations as a student. And I have imagined you in higher duties at home even as you wound up your diplomatic missions abroad. But death has unleashed its worst by cutting down my *iroko* at the most unsuspecting of times.

Your good name speaks for you, brother. Your eternity lies not only in heaven, but also in the countless documents and works you have done for our National posterity. Your faith was not second to anything including your extensive work. And now that your work is done here, I can only bid you farewell, but with the heaviest of heart and most confusing of minds.

Adieu big brother. Kindly welcome me at the end of my journey here too, just as you did in Hong Kong, in New York and in the Presidential wing of Murtala Mohammed International Airport, Lagos. Till then, your memory lives on.

The First, the Only and the Last Encounter with Osy!
Rev. Fr. Conrad Ukozor

Our brother, St. Paul, recapitulated in the scriptures that in every situation, we give glory to God, whether in joy or in sorrow. Therefore, I give glory to God that Amb. Ositadinma Anaedu (EBUBEDIKE) has left this suffering world to join the saints in heaven.

EBUBEDIKE, my first and last encounter with you was at your death bed on the 9th of December, 2022, in the Hospital at Mabushi, Abuja, to hear your confession, pray for you and give you the Viaticum, shortly before your death. I knew it would be the last time, because I felt it after leaving the hospital. After

95

hearing your confession, it was an emotional encounter with you as you were answering all the questions I was asking you, I could see tears in your eyes. I knew you desired to live because you knew you were already in good terms with the Lord, but He desired your soul to return to Him. Moreover, as the Latin saying goes *"vita mutatur, non tollitur"* meaning *"life is changed, not ended"*, you left this hostile world to enjoy with the heavenly hosts the fruits of your labour because you live on.

My brother priest, Fr. Paulinus, I commiserate with you and your siblings at this glorious *cum* mournful period. It is always painful to lose one's sibling irrespective of the age, because I have witnessed such, but be consoled that God knows what is best for him. He has called him to His Mountain in other to prepare goodies for him and to remove any garment of sickness, pain and gloom. (cf. Isaiah 25:6-8).

Ebubedike has joined the saints to intercede for you all.

Rest in peace Osy until we meet to part no more.

To a Great and Wonderful in-law
The Ogbuewu family

Osy b'anyi, it still feels surreal to know that you are no longer amongst us here physically. It still seems like a dream, yet it's true. Haa! *Ọnwọ asọ anya*! A colossus, a quintessential and complete gentleman! Very wise with words and knowledgeable! *Ifemelu! Oke ogo anyị! Jee nke ọma!*

Our father, your father-in-law, is still not the same. Who would be? Losing his beloved wife of more than 50 years and his precious son-in-law within a space of eight months. When your calls to him stopped, he became worried. No matter what and how we twisted excuses, he was adamant that we should explore more, that something wasn't right. You had always called him at a certain hour unbeknownst to us. He always looked forward to talking with you and suddenly, that call stopped. That convinced him that all wasn't well. Every night, he says his rosary diligently for the repose of your beautiful soul and that of his wife. That's the first thing he says anytime he wants to talk about you. He says, *all I ask God is to grant your soul and his wife's peaceful repose in His bosom.*

Ebubedike, you affectionately called me *Eli b'anyi*, coming up with your jokes and boisterous laughter. I miss those moments sorely. You always had wise words and advice to give. You were indeed a breath of fresh air.

You so much knew the importance of family and what our sister meant to us. You always allowed her to travel home first with the children so as to spend time with our parents before coming home to your house. We deeply appreciated that gesture, but it showed the kind of man you were. Deeply thoughtful and thinking about others always.

Your love for healthy living was extended to us – sending nuts and other healthy stuff to our parents, advising and always enquiring to see that we were on track. This life is nothing. We do our stuff and God does the rest. For it is unthinkable that sickness will take you home with all the efforts you poured into healthy living and exercising. Indeed, we all come from God and unto Him shall we all return. He alone has the keys, the time and date. We offer Him praise for the gift of you; for being a part of our family, your family and to the world at large.

Oke Ogo anyi, we say fare thee well, until that day in paradise when we all shall reunite to the glory of God. Ije oma, ezigbo ogo anyi! May the Angels receive you in paradise and please keep a watchful eyes on our daughter and sister, Amaka, and your two precious children – Kamto and Kosi. We love you, but God loves you the most. Otherwise, how could He have called you home when you were desperately needed here, when our sister and your children needed you the most?

Ambassador Ositadinma Anaedu – A rare Gem
Uche Odozor
MD/CEO Diplomatic Village, Abuja

It is with deep sadness that we pen down this tribute of the passing of Ambassador Ositadinma Anaedu, who till his death was a brother, ally and confidant. We join today friends and all members of the Nigerian Diplomatic Community to send our deepest condolences to Late Ambassador Osy Anaedu's wife and children, family, friends and indeed the Government of the Federal Republic of Nigeria at this difficult time. We mourn with you and celebrate the extraordinary life of this remarkable Ambassador who devoted his life to his family, serving God and humanity in a very unique way.

Ambassador Osy, as I fondly called him, lived a life worthy of emulation. His infectious attitude and attributes come from a humble background despite his popularity. He impacted our lives and that of many who encountered him at the Diplomatic Village. Despite his busy schedules occasioned by his dedication to service, the late Ambassador Anaedu was a high value partner and mentor, whose invaluable encouragement contributed immensely to the realization of the vision of our reputable organization.

In the passing away of Ambassador Osy Anaedu, I must say that Nigeria has lost a notable gentleman and a rare gem; we truly will miss you. We will hold dear to our hearts the great memories of your last days with us.

May God grant your soul heavenly peace and we pray that your beloved wife, children, brothers and sisters are comforted on this immeasurable loss. Adieu, Your Excellency!

A Good Friend
Rev. Fr. Dr. John Umeojiakor

There is always time to be born and time to die. So it is with you, dear Amb. Osita Anaedu. Yes, you wanted to live and continue your good work both in your family, your town, your country and in foreign affairs offices in foreign countries where you were tirelessly protecting our battered image. Death comes when it will. That is why we are now instead of visiting you, we are bidding you farewell.

As many people know, you loved yourself, your family, your friends, and humanity at large. You would have loved to continue to express your appreciation of good things when they are done well and your frustration about things that are bad. Having known you for a long time now, I can remember how welcoming you always were when I visited your family in Switzerland and your office in New York. We shared our worldviews on many things which were understandably alike in so many areas and still differ in many others. I will confess that I will miss your in-depth analysis of some serious matters in order to arrive at your conclusions about them.

Having been a good brother, husband, father, and friend here on earth, you will definitely meet your likes there in heaven. As we weep here for loosing you to them, they will equally rejoice to have you among them over there. Adieu Osy, adieu a good Christian. Be with God till we meet again.

Living in a Daze without Osy
Mazi Anekamobi Onyenwe & Lady Oby Onyenwe (nee Onyeguili), Agụlụzgbo
and
Mr. Lazarus Okammor & Mrs. Nkiru Okammor (nee Onyenwe), Enugwuagị dị

Osy, as if in a transcendental format, from your loving Dad, Late Paulinus Ọnwụzuligbo Anaedu and from your own close ties and links with us – we are undoubtedly sure that you are now smiling at us from your everlasting happy and peaceful abode in the eternal kingdom of our Father Almighty, as you always did when you were physically here with us 'yesterdays and years.' We loved and appreciated you and still do because your lifestyle and legacy had all around them testimonies as an ambassador of Christ and evidence of saintly living: faith, love, joy, peace, patience, tolerance, sincerity, good will, humanitarianism, philanthropy and intellectuality. As an ambassador, you visited our people, the Nigerians, in many parts of the world and kept healthy and peaceful relations between them and their host countries. You were a model worthy of emulation. Your absence leaves us in a daze of lurid enigma and agitation which can be resolved only by our Father Almighty. Yes, but we are sure of one thing – that God, Our Father, *Chukwu Onyeokike*, who knows us individually, will not fail to reward you for your kindness and love for your people.

To our dear brother, friend, in-law, uncle, cousin, international icon, mentor to our children and the youths, may you rest in peace as you have gone to be with our Creator Amen! Amen!! Amen!!! You will be missed. Adieu until we meet again!

Blessed are those who die in the Lord.
Lady Oby Vero Onyenwe
President General, Life Member of CWO Awka
Diocese
Chairlady Agụlụzigbo Teachers Union (ATU)

As the early morning comes and goes and as the sun keeps rising in the east with an unchanging destiny to calmly set in the west in the evening, so does the Creator of mortal beings, all flesh and bones, pronounce a time for our existence on earth to cease without any question or hesitation.

Death – despite its callousness defying all human passionate appeal: *Ọnwụbiko, Ọnwụegbuzina, Ọnwụsogbulu, Ọnwụlobelu, Ọnwụakalia, Ọnwụchekwa, Ọnwụozugo, Ọnwụmeebele, Ọnwụemelie* – continues to leave an impromptu, painful, and shattering footprint on its mortal pathway and on the sands of time that can never be averted or erased. This time it came beckoning on our noble brother, Ambassador Osy; snatching him unceremoniously away from us.

Beloved brother, your sudden disembarkment from the train of life without any valedictory ritual left us with choking discomfort and waves of sorrow, thereby, creating a laceration in us. We, in a flashback, going down memory lane, remember with sorrow, the bitter relics of your numerous, conspicuous contributions not only at the *Ụmụnna* – Ụzụanụnụ, St. Patrick's C.W.O., St Patrick's Parish, Agụlụzigbo, but also beyond the geographical entity of Nigeria.

Ambassador, you were one of the life wires in Agụlụzigbo. You were known for your positive, thoughtful contributions, hardwork and humanitarianism in Agụlụzigbo; you provided educational, social, psychological, financial succor to many youths through scholarship packages; a passionate philanthropist to the core; an international icon. The silver cup you donated to the CWO has gone a long way to the upliftment of women empowerment.

Oh Life! Looking backwards and forward, one is prompted to rhetorically ask: *what is life after all?* Vanity upon vanity; all is vanity (v*anitas vanitatum et omnia vanitas*), and that is life!!! *"Sometimes you see me, other times you will not see me,"* said Jesus Christ to his apostles. Sometimes, one is there! At other times, one is not there anymore!! But then, others keep struggling to be, to exist and to die off.

Noble brother, in the thoughts of men and women, who are the control house of their being, you were a man of many values. You demonstrated your spirituality of purpose – the ability to serve your God in all ramifications, odds, mountains, bumps, valleys, tribulations, obstacles and challenges not withstanding till your last days. Gone you are, yes! But the memories and legacies you left behind epitomize your person and presence among us and will ever remain green, not only in our hearts, in Agụlụzigbo, but also on the sands of time.

Nwoke oma, as you have alighted from the train of this life, we pray that God – who slept in the flesh and raised those who were sleeping from the ages; that God who died in the flesh and the underworld trembled, the avamalock world disintegrated; that God, whom you dedicatedly, tirelessly and zealously served – to reward you with unending victory in Jesus name, amen!

You came! You saw!! And you conquered!!! In similar mode, Osy, you fought a good fight! You kept the faith till your last breath!! Now is your crown of endless glory in Jesus name, amen!!!

Ezi nwanne, we weep for your exit from the train of life, but we then thank God for you and we are proud of the edified legacy that you left behind not only on Agụlụzigbo soil but on the totality of human-ity. Ambassador per excellence, you were a gentle lamb, down to earth, your status not-withstanding, pious to the core, a humanist – people oriented, and above all Christ-centered.

Adieu, noble brother! Adieu Ambassador! Adieu man of valor! Adieu man of integrity and substance! We celebrate you today, all to the glory of God through Christ our Lord, Amen! Amen!! Amen!!!

Evergreen in the Memory
Anaedu Fidelis for Nwachukwu Anaedu family

Evergreen in my memory. I'm so speechless, still speechless because am short of words, indeed life is a mystery. On that fateful day, I was disturbed, but l never knew that day was the last day. It sounded like a super story to me and I couldn't believe that you had gone. Oh! Death has decided to take you away from us but all I know is that God knows the best. You left a good legacy, a legacy of love, kindness, gen-erosity and others. Your memory will never be for-gotten. Ebubedike, may the good Lord grant your gentle soul an everlasting peace. Amen.

Gone too soon but marked with the Sign of Faith
Msgr Obiora Ike

Osita Anaedu left this world in a dramatic manner, putting many of his friends and family in wonder and

105

awe. Death was the last thing anyone close to or around him contemplated at his young age merely in his mid-sixties. He had been sick quite alright but not that it was for him to depart this world suddenly on that fateful Sunday morning.

The news of his death spread like wild fire bringing cold shrills and shudder at how this could happen, without notice, without ponder, without any serious long term signal... Just like that!

But Osita Anaedu had listed to and read the words of the master Jesus Christ who always admonished his followers that death comes as a thief in the night when no one ever expected. Therefore staying alert always remained the best manner to overcome death. Osita was always ready. He had premonitions that his time on earth was gradually winding down. His spirituality and nearness to his creator by living a virtuous Christian life was intensive, especially during those last months.

Covid-19 had struck the world for much of 2020 to 2022 restricting global movements of people. For some of us who belonged to two worlds, and living in Geneva and Nigeria, his physical presence in Geneva got reduced. And it meant that those many discussions I held with him and his family also reduced. Telephone discussions were not the same thing as sharing the same physical space.

I remember my last visit with him in his Geneva home in the summer of 2021 when we stood under the tree of his garden for two hours ruminating on the four last fundamental things of life - death, judgment, heaven and hell. In that discussion he made me understand that we should all be ready to die at any time if God beckons. I kept on wondering what his message was during that discussion in his home. Thereafter he gave me his newest book, a compendium of over 600 pages beautifully written with content on balance of mind and soul and body, expressing thereby and for posterity, his faith and life believing in God's goodness. That book: *Your Microbiome (Bacteria) Is A Wonder of Nature: Activate & Optimize Eating For Healthy Longevity* is a legacy which all should read. His mastery of biblical and natural sciences was enigmatic. His precision at analysing issues was rare. His intellect alert and seldom.

Osita was one person who chose his words and stood for his principles. He believed in God and the message of truth preached by the Catholic Church. He believed in humanity and reasoned that values-driven lifestyles with morality as compass was the best way to live. He abhorred dishonesty and untruth and was uncompromising to diplomatic shenanigans.

As an Ambassador of Nigeria to the United Nations and the various international institutions that make laws or guidelines for humanity based, in some cases, on Western dominated worldviews being imposed on the rest of the world, Osita Anaedu stood tall and carried many African votes to join with him in protest. And he won each time!

A force to reckon with, he protested half-truths that distorted the authentic nature and anthropology of human beings, standing contrary to the current to advocate for the dignity of persons, the moral value of existence, the equality of all human beings and the beauty in respecting African cultural values which some western diplomats desired to erase by imposing strange ideological and gender theories that contradicted and distorted the nature and originality of humanity created by a supreme God.

Osita Anaedu answered the divine call peacefully in a Sunday morning while we were in touch. His wife, Amaka, got the message that he had died peacefully, after having attended mass that Sunday and prayed for him. We all miss him but we still feel grateful that we knew him.

My condolences to his wife, Amaka, and their young children. Our time together in Geneva was like family.

He now rests in peace and has gone before us marked with the sign of faith. Requiescat in pace!

Osy, an Ambassador of Christ
Rev. Fr Martin C. Añusi
St Michael the Archangel Catholic Church, SMACC,
Eziaja, Neni, Nigeria

Reading through what people who knew him and worked with him all through his professional career said of him, leaves no one in doubt about the greatness of this mortal, Osy (that was how I had always fondly known him).

Honestly, I felt the pride of knowing such a great and an accomplished diplomat. I was also surprised because I never knew that *"Osy b'any"* was such a renowned and internationally acclaimed figure. Perhaps, the reason was that those moments I had the occasion to chat or discuss with him, we had talked more often about the mission of the Church in the world, and the enormous responsibilities of the priest in getting that mission accomplished accordingly in a way that adequately responds to the signs of the times.

Osy was in my eyes, therefore, an ardent believer in God. Perhaps it was that great faith of his in God that led to one of his outstanding successes in the United Nations, when he championed and led African group of ambassadors, other Asian and some Latino countries to fight against lesbian/gay rights and same sex marriage in 2012. He won!

One thing you would enjoy in Ossy was that he was a great conversationalist, enlightened and a great listener. His thoughts were deep, fertile, and versatile.

Do I have to talk about his generosity? That would be a story for another time. Visit his house, you will never feel as if you were in another person's home. And he had a wife, Amaka, who clearly fitted into that homely welcome to their home. I remember vividly the last I visited his house at No. 2 Tubor City Place on 41st/42nd Ave, in Manhattan, NY, on Wednesday, August 22, 2012.

Osy loved God. He loved people. He lived for other's happiness. He lived and worked for the common good. These will surely be key parts of his legacies.

Adieu Ossy! And may God reward your generosity with His (Lk. 6:38).

Fare Thee Well, Osy
Fr Prof. Chukwuemenam Umezinwa
(Vice-chancellor, Peter University
Achina/Onneh)

With hallows on his head and all the trappings of greatness, Osy was a brilliant diplomat, a detached soul, a silent achiever and a consummate orator.

To those who admired him, he was a quintessential gentleman. To those who saw life as competition for money, power and hubris, he took no notice. Towards them that wished him evil, he felt no bitterness.

Since his soul was not earthbound, he refused the relentless provocations from every axis of evil; and while keeping his gaze on the starry heavens, he conquered the fear of living or dying.

Very few men have attained and sustained such heights with a consistency which neither evil nor good could derail. Fare thee well, Ambassador Osy!